"This welcome book blends sound biblical truth and solid psychology to tackle those problems of troublesome emotions and unhelpful thoughts. Clear and practical, this is a book to be read, re-read and acted on."

CANON J.JOHN
Author, broadcaster and evangelist

"Jo's faith, honesty and expertise have come together powerfully in *Disentangled*. She shows us a way to stop avoiding feelings and thoughts in the safety of God's grace and sovereignty, and follows this with practical steps. If you don't know where to start with spiritual formation because your thoughts and feelings seem too scary, then I would highly recommend starting here!"

KRIS DEFRIEND
Retired child and adolescent psychiatrist

"Our personal thoughts and feelings hold more currency today than perhaps at any other time in history. While these internal narratives form an important part of the way God made us, Jo Johnson helpfully and expertly shows us that there is more to this story. She exhorts us to remember the truths of Scripture and of who we are in Christ rather than reverting to quick, automatic conclusions about ourselves and others. This book deftly and carefully brings together the best of what we know of psychological theory with the unchanging truths of God's word—equipping every follower of Jesus with an opportunity to pursue a path of increased consciousness, measure and ultimately Christ-likeness."

CHRIS CIPOLLONE
Founding Director, Life to the Full

Disentangled

© Jo Johnson, 2026

Published by:
The Good Book Company

thegoodbook.com | thegoodbook.co.uk
thegoodbook.com.au | thegoodbook.co.nz

Unless indicated, all Scripture references are taken from the Holy Bible, New International Version. Copyright © 2011 Biblica. Used by permission.

All rights reserved. Except as may be permitted by the Copyright Act, no part of this publication may be reproduced in any form or by any means without prior permission from the publisher.

Jo Johnson has asserted her right under the Copyright, Designs and Patents Act 1988 to be identified as author of this work.

Every book published by The Good Book Company has been written by a human author and edited by a human editor. While AI tools are sometimes used to assist with research and support certain processes, all content has been created by a human author and thoroughly checked by our editorial team.

Cover design by Studio Gearbox | Art direction and design by André Parker

ISBN: 9781802543780 | JOB-008382 | Printed in India

JO JOHNSON

DIS ENTAN GLED

Taming your **thoughts** and **feelings** to live **freely** for **Jesus**

thegoodbook COMPANY

This book is dedicated to my almighty God of grace, peace and compassion.

To Jesus, who saved me when psychology couldn't, and to his Spirit, who changed me from the inside out.

Last and least, to Lyndon Johnson, who continues to show me what my Servant King's heart looks like on a camera.

CONTENTS

DEAR READER...

This morning almost started well. When I opened my eyes, I offered a prayer of gratitude for a new day and a warm house. "At last, I'm learning to be content," I thought. But immediately, my husband ruined it. I had to get up, but he was still asleep and wasn't breathing quietly! I deliberately yanked the duvet as I got up.

"How is this fair?" I seethed.

"All right for you," I grumbled.

Struggling in the dimly lit hall, I tripped over my daughter's bag. "Clear up after yourself!" I ranted inwardly.

Before long, even the cheap kettle had got a rant for its slow boiling.

"Maybe I'd be happier living alone," I thought.

The kitchen clock chimed 6 a.m. The day had barely begun and already a monster was on the loose. I slumped into a heap, feeling utterly despondent. *This is not who I want to be. Surely this isn't who I am?*

As a clinical neuropsychologist, I'm supposed to be the expert, but despite five decades of life, you can see I remain a deeply flawed, moderately messed-up muddle of a human. Like most of us, I hope others won't see my true nature if I paste on a smile, wear clean clothes and work hard at church. Sadly, that isn't true. In the face of the smallest struggle, the truth is shown by my actions.

But it's not how we want to be, is it? I desperately want to be a supportive wife. I want to be a loving mum, a kind colleague and the most grateful friend. I want to be seen as joyful, sunny and easy to please. I want to be remembered as someone who exemplifies the love of Jesus.

So, why am I grumpy and irritable at the smallest problem? Why do I withdraw when I want to have fun? Why am I mean when I want to be kind?

Why am I such a mess?

Two Kinds of Answer

When I'm asked this question at work, I explain that whether we're aware of it or not, we are frequently controlled by what's going on inside of us. Our negative thoughts and painful feelings act as internal saboteurs, which is why we so often behave like the person we least want to be.

My clinical answer explains *what* we experience as part of the normal human condition. But the Bible explains *why* this is the default human condition. We all struggle in much the same way because we've inherited Adam's weak and sinful DNA. By nature, we are unable to be good because we are not good. We are sinners.

Sometimes, of course, we do better. We help out even though we'd rather watch Netflix. We take criticism with humility and respond well when we envy. In these moments, we feel like the rational, spiritual people we were created to be. We experience the sweet spot we've been designed to enjoy.

But our best moments are less frequent than we'd like. So, how do we manage our inner turmoil and enjoy more time in the sweet spot?

Should we lie about our thoughts and feelings?

Should we try harder?

Should we use our tricky thoughts and painful feelings as an excuse to behave badly?

The reality is that there is only one true solution. Jesus lived a perfect life and gave it up for me so that I can be transformed to become like him. I am still a mess, but in Jesus, I am a *holy* mess. One day, I'll leave my mess and enjoy being forever holy.

My job as a clinical psychologist is to help people spend more time in the "sweet spot". I teach them the skills to manage their thoughts, feelings and desires so that their behaviour starts to match up with how they want to be, and they can live the lives they want.

As a Christian, I also know that in order to see the deepest change, we need God to be at work in our lives. We need to be transformed from within. Then our outer behaviour will not just reflect who we want to be but who God wants us to be.

But this transformation we need from God doesn't mean that the skills I teach as a psychologist are not relevant for believers. They are! Even as Christians, we get distracted. We forget what Jesus has done for us, or we stop following in his ways, and consequently we end up burnt out, or withdrawing from people because we can't cope.

The Bible urges us "to put off your old self"—which you might call the messy self—"to be made new in the attitude of your minds; and to put on the new self, created to be like God in true righteousness and holiness" (Ephesians 4:22-24). *Put off* and *put on*. As Christians, we have been given a new self by the work of Jesus—but we still have to put it on every day. And here is where the tools of psychology can help.

A Book for You

I don't know what attracted you to this title; maybe you struggle with your inner mess or someone you love needs help. Maybe you enjoy a calm mind, or maybe, like me, you're an overthinker. Maybe you feel fine, or maybe you feel frazzled. Whatever your reasons or situation, this book is for all of us.

I am a Christian writing for Christians, but if you are a non-believer, please don't go. Within this book, I make theological assumptions that you may not agree with, but I invite you to read on, asking yourself, "Does this match what I observe in the world around me? Could this be true?" In the first line of John's Gospel in the Bible, Jesus is described as the word of God—or in the original Greek, the *logos* of God. This is where we get the word "logic". I'm convinced that Jesus is the logic: with him everything else makes sense. He offers the inner peace we all crave.

I trust you will find something useful in these pages.

How to Use This Book

I have a friend who always reads the last chapter of a book before starting it. As for me, I sometimes read non-fiction like a recipe book. I just read the pages I like the look of. With this book, though, both of those reading strategies will sadly fail you.

Each chapter builds on the previous one, and most chapters will include a reflection theme or a skill to practise. The tools promoted in Part 1 build upon the ideas described in Part 2. Go at your own pace, making sure you've grasped the ideas in each chapter before running to the next.

While I hope this book will help you as an individual, you might enjoy reading it with others. Consider working through it with a prayer partner, in a small group or with a church leader you trust.

PART ONE

RUNNING THE RACE

CHAPTER 1

AN INNER WORLD

You're probably wondering, "Who is this Jo Johnson?" and "Can a psychologist be trusted?" Perhaps you fear this book will be psychobabble with a smattering of Bible verses. I hope you'll soon feel reassured.

Years ago, when I started my psychology degree, a number of Christians expressed concern. They felt it was misguided to study psychology. They felt it was anti-faith. They were concerned I would lose my way, believing that self-help or therapy can resolve my inner mess when only Jesus can do that.

When I started my clinical psychology training, many of my colleagues thought that Christians were stupid, that God was a fairy tale and that psychology could resolve everyone's problems.

Sadly, for years I was scared to talk of psychology in church and scared to talk of Jesus at work! But after 30 years of being a psychologist, I'm more convinced than ever that I can be a Christian psychologist. I've read hundreds of books describing the human disposition, and I can confidently assert that the Bible narrative is the best explanation of what I've read—and what I see and hear in my clinical practice.

An Inner World

Yesterday, I bumped into a lady who introduced herself as Claire. We were in a bookshop chatting about novels. When she found out I was a psychologist, she opened up, as many people do. She said, "I am an overthinker. I'm needy. I feel anxious a lot. I don't think people like me. I can be really spiteful. Do you think I have mental issues?"

Claire is not alone. Many people feel so overwhelmed by their inner world that they worry they're somehow abnormal. They're wrong. In a given day, the average brain produces 60,000 thoughts, a roller coaster of emotions and a vast array of desires. All of this is a gift from God! Our complex inner life is one of the things that makes us human and differentiates us from all other creatures. But sometimes this can get tricky.

I was able to reassure Claire that she is much the same as me. She is much the same as my friends. She is much the same as most of us.

Or maybe you're not quite like Claire and me. You're not having endless conversations in your head, you're unaware of any painful emotions, and you just get on with things. Let me assure you, everyone has an inner world. Sadly, being less aware of your inner content doesn't reduce your chances of being thrown off course by it.

Pause for a moment.

What can you hear? Where are you?

What are you thinking?

How are you feeling physically? Are you tired, restless, hungry or uncomfortable?

Can you notice any emotions? Maybe you're feeling anxious or sad? Maybe today is a good day, and you are full of joy. Maybe you're irritated, frustrated or fed up.

Right now, are you longing for a coffee and cake, or do you fancy a run?

For now, what you're thinking, feeling or craving doesn't matter very much. But whatever is going on, you're glimpsing your inner world: the non-physical or psychological part of you. Our inner world allows us to taste, see, smell, focus, remember the past, imagine, problem-solve, plan for the future and connect with others. It's amazing!

Our inner worlds are all different. I have fast access to thoughts and words, whereas my husband is a slow, clear thinker who finds it hard to express himself. Some people experience frequent ups and downs, whereas others are mostly on an even keel. Some are prone to stress and anxiety, whereas others are often frustrated and quick-tempered. These are *all* variations of a normal post-Fall disposition.

As part of our physical experience, we have aches and pains, coughs, colds and headaches. Something similar is true of our psychological experience. There will be days when we feel tearful, low or anxious, and other times when we find it hard to concentrate. These are normal psychological aches, pains and sniffles.

As with physical illness, Christians are as vulnerable to mental illness as non-Christians; but most people reading this book will have an inner life that is well within the normal range. Our inner struggles are a part of our shared human experience—they are mostly not symptoms of mental illness.

A Biblical Self-Image

Sadly, many Christians feel the same as Claire—they must be abnormal—but with the added fear that their messy inner lives indicate a lack of salvation. But we should resist this. When writing in the New Testament, Paul felt comfortable revealing his inner struggles and the impact it had on his behaviour. He felt no need to cover up or lie. Here's what he says in Romans 7:15-19:

> *I do not understand what I do. For what I want to do I do not do, but what I hate I do ... For I have the desire to do what is good, but I cannot carry it out. For I do not do the good I want to do, but the evil I do not want to do—this I keep on doing.*

Paul expresses what we so often feel. I want to be a good mum, but I shout at my kids. I want to be a loyal friend, but I get irritated and frustrated. I want to be in church, but I long for the protection of home. However, Paul doesn't question his sanity or his salvation. He doesn't fear what others might think or feel the need to pretend that he's perfect. Why? Because the way he sees himself is determined by the Bible.

What we believe about our inner mess is vitally important. The secular view is that we are mostly good but occasionally slip up. The Bible says the opposite! A biblical self-image means knowing that we are made in the image of God and are thus capable of great good, but that our default is to do wrong. Until we are comfortable with this uncomfortable truth, we won't submit to the Holy Spirit's transforming power. We will keep trying to do better but fail and end up in self-defeating cycles. If even Paul, a Bible writer, couldn't perfect his behaviour, there's not much hope for us!

Having a biblical self-image enabled Paul to be emotionally honest with God and others. If we are unable to be honest about our messy inner lives, we will live in fear of being exposed; we will lie to ourselves and hide from God. Our resulting behaviour will be self-protective, defensive and withdrawn. Or self-promoting, critical and boastful.

Where does that leave us—should we just give up? Absolutely not. If we are followers of Jesus, we have the Holy Spirit as our truthful coach and biblical counsellor. He is always on our side and endlessly willing and patient. He longs for us to reflect God to a world in despair. In order for our actions to be fruitful, we have to submit our inner lives to the Spirit and then learn the skills that will help us relate differently to our unruly internal teenagers.

Parenting Your Inner Self

I sometimes work with teenagers who are behaving badly. Often, these are children who have too much control within their family. They are unruly because they're feeling overwhelmed, tired and anxious. When their exhausted parents learn to relate differently to their child, the behaviour often resolves.

Our thoughts, feelings and desires are similar to children. They are gifts that can bless us. But they create carnage and exhaust us when they are allowed to rule the roost! So, our inner lives need to be effectively parented—listened to but not given too much control.

Imagine you are babysitting a little girl. First you need to notice that she's present. Then you have to pay her careful attention. When she cries or throws a tantrum, you have to stop what you're doing and investigate. Perhaps she's hurt or tired, and you can calm her with an obvious solution. When you realise she's making a big fuss because she desires the bright red chilli in the fridge, you can safely tell her no and get on with something more important.

Thoughts and feelings are just the same: they need to be first noticed, then given attention and then intentionally managed.

Feelings on Camera

This really matters, as what goes on inside of us—our beliefs, our thoughts, our memories, our feelings and our desires—impacts everything we do and how well we do it. Our inner lives determine how we show up in a given moment and whether we'll behave as we'd like or not.

Have a read of the scenarios on the next page. They are all based on stories people have shared with me.

It's not even big things that trigger our inner struggles, is it? All through each day, we experience thoughts which trigger feelings of anxiety, self-doubt, jealousy or rejection, which in turn trigger difficult thoughts and feelings about God, ourselves and others. And this in turn

	Situation	**Thoughts**
Simon	A helper at church has reordered the chairs.	Who does he think he is? I'm the only one who can do this right.
Leon	His moody teen has a tantrum.	What's the point? I need me time! I've failed as a dad!
Emily	Her husband asks her for help.	How dare he? What about me?
Tim	He watches the collection bag circulate.	Why should I give? He's rich—he should put in more!
Kelly	The preacher says we should practise hospitality.	But I'm busy. It's my life, and the football is on. I deserve a rest.
Aidan	Traffic is slow.	That old man is driving slowly on purpose. What an idiot! Everything goes wrong for me.
Sofia	She sits on her own at church.	I'm left out. No one likes me. I might as well go home.

leads to actions that are unhelpful or even sinful. You can see that if not well parented, our thoughts and feelings have great potential to lead us into trouble.

I sometimes ask people what they might see if their behaviour was being recorded on CCTV. What do your thoughts and feelings look like on a camera? In other words, what actions do they lead to?

If you observed me on a camera, you'd notice that when I'm tired, anxious or bored, I reach for chocolate. When I feel insecure or left out, I withdraw to my iPad. When my body feels restless and anxious, I talk too much or berate my husband. When I feel a failure, I am quiet.

Think about the scenarios above—what do they look like on camera? Aidan is winding himself up into an angry frenzy. Emily is getting irritable. Sofia will go home and miss out on fellowship at church. How might Leon or Simon feel if they believe their thoughts, and how will they respond? What about Tim—will he give generously? Will Kelly obey the biblical command to be hospitable?

Our thoughts and feelings are inside, but they show on the outside. Sometimes the way they show is simply unhelpful to us (like being quiet and withdrawn when it would be better for me to engage with people). Sometimes it's sinful (like berating my husband when he doesn't deserve it). Unhelpful or sinful behaviours are symptoms of an inner life that needs work—thoughts and feelings that need to be parented. This is why, ultimately, a change of behaviour is not what's needed. It's a change of heart.

In Matthew 15, as usual, Jesus' critics are resentful, bitter and desperate for power. Their inner lives show in their camera behaviour: they are complaining. They are judging the disciples for breaking religious rules about cleanliness and food (v 1-2).

Jesus declares that our problem isn't what goes *into* the mouth but what comes *out* of it (v 11)!

The disciples ask him to explain. I love his response.

> *"Are you still so dull?" Jesus asked them ... "The things that come out of a person's mouth come from the heart, and these defile them. For out of the heart come evil thoughts—murder, adultery, sexual immorality, theft, false testimony, slander." (v 16, 18-19)*

Jesus is saying that sin starts inside.

Change is Possible

So often, our inner lives lead us into unhappiness and away from right living. This process is so automatic that we are often unaware that our inner lives are the strings and we are the helpless puppets! But this doesn't *have* to happen. We *can* parent our inner lives better than this.

As Paul writes about the frustration of not doing the good he wants to do, he finishes with a cry for help: "Who will rescue me from this body that is subject to death?" (Romans 7:24). It sounds hopeless. But immediately Paul reveals that he does have a saviour—someone who is helping him to live in the way he wants to live.

> *Thanks be to God, who delivers me through Jesus Christ our Lord! (v 25)*

Just like Paul, those of us who trust in Christ have been gifted the Holy Spirit: God's presence living in us. The mind controlled by the Spirit is life and peace (Romans 8:6). Because of what Jesus has achieved, we *can* live in a way that is pleasing to God! It's the Spirit's job to transform our inner lives—we just have to be willing to partner with him.

The psychological ideas I use to help people manage their unruly thoughts, feelings and desires are from a model of therapy called Acceptance and Commitment Therapy (ACT). ACT is a good abbreviation, as this therapy is about taking action. ACT gives people the tools to move towards their values (the commitment component) by noticing and relating differently to their thoughts, feelings and desires (the acceptance component).

I started using ACT-informed tools over a decade ago. The tools made me aware of unhelpful thoughts and feelings, so that I wasn't puppeted into sinful behaviours. I have since shared these tools with many Christians who have enjoyed the same benefit.

Does this mean my own inner life exemplifies perfection? Does this mean all my thoughts are positive and what I feel is righteous and proportionate? Does this mean I always behave in a God-honouring way? Definitely not! I have a long-standing struggle with anxiety and jealousy, and a tendency towards self-doubt. I struggle in groups, am over-sensitive when criticised, feel vulnerable to rejection and am more self-righteous than a Pharisee.

I write this book not as an expert but as a messy disciple who longs to be more like Jesus.

It's him we're going to think about in our next chapter.

Time to Reflect

At the end of each chapter, this book will invite you to pause.

Each morning, most of us look in the mirror. We look intently to ensure we haven't got toast in our hair or egg on our face. If we took only a brief glimpse, we'd be in danger of looking foolish—going out as if we had a clean face when we didn't.

The Bible is intended to be a soul mirror.

> *Anyone who listens to the word but does not do what it says is like someone who looks at his face in a mirror and, after looking at himself, goes away and immediately forgets what he looks like. (James 1:23)*

We are not supposed to skim-read a few verses, forget what we've read and consequently remain unchanged. The word of God is intended to produce heart change that shows in our actions.

So, at the end of each chapter, I'll offer a biblical truth to embed in your mind. A challenge for your heart.

I'll also recommend a song to sing. While it might at first seem strange, singing aloud has many benefits, especially when it's intended as an act of worship. Singing regulates our breathing, thus calming bodily anxiety, and is an easy way to memorise biblical truth, making it accessible in times of trouble. Even if, like me, your singing talent is minimal, you can still make a joyful noise to the Lord!

So, here goes your first pause for a look in God's mirror.

Pause for a Look in God's Mirror

First, still yourself before God. Take notice of a few breaths. Listen to what you can hear. Notice what you can smell and see.

Prayerfully read Psalm 139. Praise God for the inner life you've been gifted.

Reflect on the last few weeks. Remember a few highlights, with a grateful heart for the ways in which your inner life enables you to enjoy God, life and relationships.

> *I praise you because I am fearfully and wonderfully made.*
> *(Psalm 139:14)*

God knows you better than you know yourself and yet loves and accepts you. He doesn't want you to hide anything from him. He knows it all anyway!

Thank God that because he knows you inside and out, you can be honest. Tell God any thoughts and feelings you've had about yourself while reading this chapter.

Invite the Spirit to give you the courage to be honest about your inner struggles and the resulting behaviours. Being emotionally honest with God will help you to be honest with yourself and others. Emotional honesty is the first step to a transformed inner life that produces fruitful behaviour.

Song to sing: *Lead Us in Your Truth* by EMU Music

Use the QR code to find a playlist of all the songs mentioned in the book, plus a discussion guide for every chapter.

CHAPTER 2

HUMANITY'S SWEET SPOT

What's your favourite designed thing? Perhaps a bike, a computer, a tool or a musical instrument? Whatever it is, I'm sure you'll know its sweet spot—what it needs in order to work well. And you'll be able to see, hear or feel when it's pushed outside of those limits. It'll overheat or slow down, or even break or be ruined.

My husband loves a fancy car! He won't be getting one anytime soon, but he stops in his tracks if he hears the gentle purr of a well-designed engine in its sweet spot.

I love Yorkshire tea! But when I forget to secure the kettle lid, it screams a loud, painful noise and fails to heat the water. Not the sweet spot.

Just like cars and kettles, us humans are *designed*. The first three chapters of the Bible reveal what our sweet spot is and what happens when we step outside of our intended limits.

God's Design for Humans

Let's consider a few moments from early on in Genesis:

> *In the beginning God created the heavens and the earth.* *(Genesis 1:1)*
>
> *Then God said, "Let us make mankind in our image, in our likeness, so that they may rule over the fish in the sea and the birds in the sky, over the livestock and all the wild animals, and over all the creatures that move along the ground." (v 26)*
>
> *So God created mankind in his own image, in the image of God he created them; male and female he created them. (v 27)*
>
> *Then the LORD God formed a man from the dust of the ground and breathed into his nostrils the breath of life, and the man became a living being. (2:7)*

Every person has been designed as a living, breathing, embodied soul in the image of God. Our designed abilities are superior to the rest of creation. We were created as men and women, complementing each other, ruling under God and reflecting his nature.

God is deeply relational—the Father has been in loving and intimate relationship with the Son and the Spirit, for ever. God made humans to be relational too. In a list of things that God observed to be good, Genesis 2:18 describes the only "not good": it is not good for man to be alone. We were made to relate.

Humans have been gifted with what psychologists call social cognition. This includes a set of automatic abilities that enable us to relate effectively. For example, our ability to read facial expressions and to understand and empathise with others, or our drive to show compassion. Social cognition is enabled and enhanced by our unique gift of language. No other creature can enjoy a cuppa and a chat.

So what does the story of our creation tell us about our sweet spot—the place where our inner lives find rest? Our sweet spot is when we worship our relational creator God as our ruler and Father, and when we relate to each other well.

Looking *up* to God and *out* to others: that's our designed sweet spot. Outside of these limits, we resemble a misfiring engine or a kettle with a permanently open lid!

Crashing Out of the Sweet Spot

God showed Adam and Eve that he was a good Father and that his good intentions could be trusted. He made them to image his nature and gifted them position and purpose. Everything Adam and Eve saw in creation, along with their abilities and their intimacy with each other, proved that God was telling the truth.

God said yes to all their true needs and gave them only one "no": they were not to eat from the tree of the knowledge of good and evil.

Then Satan entered the picture, determined to undermine Adam and Eve's belief in their Father God.

Take a closer look at Satan's strategic plan in Genesis 3:1-5. First, he casts doubt on God's word. "Did God really say…?" (v 1). Then he calls God a liar—claiming it isn't true that

Adam and Eve will die if they eat the fruit (v 4-5). Finally, he implies that God is being restrictive for his own good, not theirs. "God knows that when you eat from it your eyes will be opened, and you will be like God" (v 5).

This final trump card proves irresistible.

Adam and Eve are free to choose who and what they believe. Their choice will determine their behaviour—whether they obey or disobey. They choose to believe that God is unfair and not on their side, and that going their own way will bring the happiness, control and wisdom they deserve. They want more.

They seek enlightenment and good feelings. But you know the story—what do they get? They get a guilty conscience. They feel naked and ashamed of themselves in front of each other (v 7).

How do their inner feelings show on a camera? In an attempt to feel better, they cobble together a covering (v 7). But I don't imagine those flimsy fig leaves were much of a solution. Next, they hide (v 8). Finally, they each blame someone else (v 12-13). Adam blames God for giving him Eve. Eve blames the serpent. Here's the beginning of othering, self-defence and self-justification.

Is any of this ringing bells?

Unbelief yanked Adam and Eve's minds from God. That's what sin is. Sin demands, "*My* will be done" instead of "Lord God, *your* will be done". And sadly, every person born since Adam shares his DNA and (except one) follows in his footsteps. We disobey God, and we crash right out of the sweet spot.

Fearing Exposure

As part of a training programme to help people manage their inner lives, I ask participants to raise a hand if they feel they are "not good enough". Over the years, I have trained thousands of people, and almost everyone has raised a hand! We all share the same sense of somehow being "off". Our consciences confirm that we are not what we should be. Even for those who subscribe to the secular idea that people are basically good, there is something inside them that still declares, "Guilty".

Our greatest fear is that no one else feels the same. We long to love and be loved, but we fear our inner mess will be discovered. In order to cope with these feelings of insecurity, we try all sorts of tactics. We try to convince others that we have it all sorted. We argue, we lie, we self-justify and we blame. We withdraw, or we soothe our painful feelings and accusatory thoughts with distractions like food or alcohol.

It's as if we're in a courtroom inside our heads, acting as our own defence lawyers. We all crave a "not guilty" verdict. We long to feel covered and secure! But the fig leaves we try to stitch together just don't work.

For Adam and Eve, God provided exactly what they needed. They relinquished superficial leaves to accept proper clothing—a covering God designed for them (v 21).

And we too get a perfectly designed covering for our sin: Jesus.

The Perfect Human

Jesus was fully human and had an inner life just like ours—except he did not sin. Jesus always believed that

God was good and trustworthy. The Bible doesn't usually go into detail about what Jesus was feeling and thinking, but the perfection of his thoughts, the pure motives of his heart and the goodness of his desires were all evidenced by his actions. If you could have seen Jesus' behaviour on a CCTV camera, you would have seen a man who lived in willing submission to his Father, with a heart that looked out towards others. *Up* and *out*: that's the sweet spot all humans were designed to occupy.

Jesus regularly referred to doing what the Father wanted him to (John 4:34; 5:30; 6:39). He said that his Father's will was his food, his purpose and his work. This was evidenced when he frequently retreated to pray. Jesus always looked up. That gave him the right perspective to look out and serve others.

Even when he was tired or on his way somewhere, Jesus made time to bless and minister to the weak, the poor, foreigners and the broken. He didn't tolerate injustice or hypocrisy, but when he felt frustrated or disappointed, he told the truth without losing control or doing wrong.

Mark 14:32-36 gives us what is probably our clearest glimpse of Jesus' inner world, and it's in turmoil. He is in the Garden of Gethsemane, and he knows that the climax of his Father's plan is drawing near. Jesus will soon die. He is desperate and distressed.

Jesus cries out to his Father and begs him to take away what is about to happen. Yet even in his worst hour, Jesus still believes that his Father knows best. Despite traumatic thoughts and feelings, he willingly submits and does what is right. He willingly offers his life.

In the New Testament, Jesus is described as the second Adam (1 Corinthians 15:45; Romans 5:12-19). The first Adam put himself first. At the first hurdle, he disbelieved God. But Jesus came to succeed where Adam failed. Jesus declared, "Not my will, but yours be done."

Jesus lived the perfect life—thinking right, feeling right and doing right. His inner life of perfection produced the fruit of the Spirit for all to see.

The Perfect Covering

Do you remember Jacob and Esau from the Old Testament? To steal the blessing that belonged to Esau, Jacob covered himself in fur, pretending to be his hairy brother. Isaac, their blind elderly father, gave his blessing to the wrong brother because Jacob was "wearing" the right brother. Jacob got the blessing his brother deserved because he was covered by what seemed like Esau's skin.

When the Bible says we are "in Christ", we can think of a similar picture. If I trust in Christ, it is as if I am "wearing" him, covered by him. Galatians 3:26-27 puts it like this:

> *So in Christ Jesus you are all children of God through faith, for all of you who were baptised into Christ have clothed yourselves with Christ.*

In Jacob's case, it was a deception. He got away with it, but he shouldn't have done it—and he must have feared being exposed as someone he wasn't. In our case, we don't need to fear. This was Jesus' plan from the start. He chose to cover us. He chose to live a perfect life on our behalf.

This means that when God, my Father, looks at me, I don't have to impress by pretending to be someone I'm not. I'm "wearing" Jesus, who has impressed him on my behalf. Because of Jesus, we can be unashamed in our Father's presence. We get the blessing that Jesus deserves.

When Jesus said, "It is finished" (John 19:30), he reversed the effects of what Adam did. A truly fitting covering is now available to sinful humans. This means that the "off" feeling can go. Our guilty conscience and the resulting shame are dealt with. Our sin—our rejection of God and the sweet spot he designed for us—is forgiven.

Back to the Sweet Spot

Once we have this covering, we can return to the way we were designed to be—looking up to God and out to others. But as we've already seen, this is a battle.

Satan hates restoration. He can't create; he can only spoil. He is anti-relationship and wants us trapped in our inner courtroom, looking *in* and *down* and doing no good.

In our struggle and failure, we keep on facing the same choice Adam and Eve faced. Will we believe that Satan's quick fixes will soothe our shame and meet our needs, and stay wrapped up in ourselves? Or will we listen to the Spirit, look up, believe God and enjoy being wrapped up in Jesus?

It's only if we choose the latter that, overflowing with thankfulness, we can use our arms, legs and voices to reflect God's acceptance, forgiveness, justice and mercy to others.

Pause for a Look in God's Mirror

Still yourself before God. Take notice of a few breaths.

Prayerfully read John 20:30-31.

Jesus lived the perfect life so we can believe that he is who he says he is, that he's done what he says he's done, and that, as a result, we are who he says we are—innocent, righteous and covered. That's having life in Jesus' name!

Each time we have inner struggles, we have Adam's choice. God says, *I am good and trustworthy. I want to do you good.* Satan says, *Me too.* Who will you believe?

Song to sing: *Before the Throne of God Above*

The second verse reflects the *up* and *out* sweet spot we were designed for. Below, I have written a parallel *in* and *down* version for you to ponder:

When Satan tempts me to despair
And tells me of the guilt within,
Inward I look and see me there;
There is no end to all my sin.
I forget the Saviour died.
I forget my soul is free.
I forget God is satisfied.
Pardon me, while off I rush to
Defend and prove myself.

But here is the original verse:

When Satan tempts me to despair
And tells me of the guilt within,

Upward I look and see him there
Who made an end to all of my sin.
Because the sinless Saviour died,
My sinful soul is counted free,
For God the just is satisfied
To look on him and pardon me,
To look on him and pardon me.

Next time you are in a place of emotional struggle, invite the Holy Spirit to help your unbelief. Reflect on being hidden in Jesus. Change your body posture to reflect a feeling of security. Look up and say thank you. Be sure that you're fully known but still loved. There is no need for the fig leaves of self-promotion or self-protection. All that is finished. Be wrapped up in Jesus!

CHAPTER 3

THE GRACE RACE

Sitting in the garden, I heard a cheer. Oscar, my son, appeared with a huge smile, waving a piece of paper. His head was high as he read with pride. "You have been accepted into the Brighton marathon—get race ready!"

I congratulated him, but I had big questions.

"Don't you have to prove you have experience?"

"Are you sure you're fit enough?"

"How much have you paid?"

Oscar looked at me with disdain. "It's completely free. I asked for a place, and they said yes."

Acceptance without proof of ability or commitment... Is that a thing?

Thankfully, it's absolutely a thing. It's called grace. Grace is acceptance before change, and it runs like a golden thread throughout the entire Bible.

My favourite parable is the story of the prodigal son in Luke 15:11-32. Jesus tells the story of a younger son who believes that the freedom he craves will be found away from the sweet spot of looking up and out. He demands to be set free from his loving father and insists on dismantling the family estate to get his share. Off he stomps without a backward glance... but it is not long before he runs out of money, thrills and friends, and in desperation takes a job feeding pigs. Hungry and tired, the son hatches a plan to get back in his father's good books. He figures out an apology speech which includes offering to work for his father as an employee to pay off his debt.

Can you imagine him? Trudging home, exhausted, ashamed and smelling of pig. Head down, full of self-doubt, ruminating over his plan, anxious it might fail.

But while the wayward son is still far off, his father, filled with compassion, runs towards him. A compassionate father who runs was unheard of in this Middle-Eastern patriarchal society! The father doesn't listen to his son's carefully rehearsed apology. Instead he covers his foul-smelling child with fine robes—not to make him look like a son but because he *is* already a son. This is grace! Can you feel it?

Jesus told this story to show his Father's heart. This is the concept of grace, personified in a God who runs to embrace those who are empty-handed, unwashed and wrapped up in themselves. It is mind-blowing.

The Rat Race and the Grace Race

What do you see as you look at the world around you?

I see tired people who long for acceptance, living in a culture that affirms an aggressive competition for more money, power and status, while simultaneously telling us we should be kind. Everyone is working harder, resting less and doing what is right in their own eyes, while being terrified they'll get cancelled for saying the wrong thing. But the right thing changes so fast that it's impossible to keep up!

No wonder modern society gets described as the rat race.

In the New Testament, the Christian life is compared to a race. But it's not a rat race. The day you believe Jesus, he rescues you from the rat race and gifts you a place in the grace race.

> *Let us run with perseverance the race marked out for us, fixing our eyes on Jesus, the pioneer and perfecter of faith. (Hebrews 12:1-2)*

This is the easy life we were designed for. Yes, I said easy. The Christian life is hard in lots of ways—it involves struggle and suffering—but there *is* a sense in which it is easy. Why? Because our shame is gone. In Jesus we get significance, security and a new inner self.

I love the way The Message, a paraphrase of the Bible, describes Jesus' invitation in Matthew 11:28-30:

> *Are you tired? Worn out? Burned out on religion? Come to me. Get away with me and you'll recover your life. I'll show you how to take a real rest. Walk with me and work with me—watch how I do it. Learn the unforced rhythms of grace. I won't lay anything heavy or ill-fitting on you. Keep company with me and you'll learn to live freely and lightly.*

We are supposed to enjoy a light yoke—an inner freedom that fills us with relief. This is what it means to be wrapped in Christ.

Not Guilty

Part of my job as a neuropsychologist is to support individuals who have suffered a catastrophic injury in an accident that wasn't their fault. The person has to provide endless evidence that they are not to blame while waiting for their case to come to court. The process is hard and often takes years.

Finally, they get a court date. They stand in the witness box. The lawyers argue until the judge brings things to a close. The verdict is "not guilty". My client will never again have to prove their innocence. Their case is finished! They are justified. They punch the air as they walk out of the Royal Courts of Justice.

Every Christian experiences something similar. Your case is finished. You walked into the court as your own advocate, but Jesus enters the witness box in your place. He is the star witness, whose evidence is so compelling that the case against you falls apart. A cheer is heard from the gallery as he gifts you the "not guilty" verdict that belongs to him.

Do you hear that? Not guilty. If you're trusting in Jesus, the old has gone. All those shameful things you've thought, felt or done: they're gone. Anything people say against you is futile. Any negative thing you believe about yourself is inadmissible evidence. You are a new person, born again with the breath of Jesus in your lungs, his life in your veins.

Do you believe that?

I want to share a verse that has helped me to visualise what experiencing God's grace is meant to feel like.

In the Old Testament, God rescued his people from

slavery. There was no further need to cower or fear being hurt. Here's what he told them:

> *I am the* L*ORD your God, who brought you out of Egypt so that you would no longer be slaves to the Egyptians; I broke the bars of your yoke and enabled you to walk with heads held high. (Leviticus 26:13)*

This picture applies to Christians too. Christ has set you free and given you a place in the grace race (Galatians 5:1). So hold your head high!

Pause for a moment. Shift your posture and notice the impact of lifting your head. You have been saved to be free of shame and self. Imagine slipping off the burden of others' opinions, your own opinion, the fear of death, the heavy cover-ups of a clean house, a good-looking body, a clever CV and endless church work. Hold your head high.

Running the Grace Race

When my son Oscar was accepted to run the marathon, he was gifted a free shirt to prove his race acceptance.

What features would our grace-race shirts include? Surely the outer layer would be pure white, representing Christ's perfect life. The lining would be velvet—soft and warm, and red, to remind us of the cost of our comfort. The lining is infused with the Spirit, who gives supernatural power whatever the hurdles. Around each sleeve is gold trim to remind us that as we walk in the Spirit, we are a glorified mess, better than we should have been. One day, we will be glorified—no mess.

Having accepted his place, Oscar was given a route map

and a code of conduct. *Stay in lane. Show respect. Stay hydrated.* There was even advice about finding a running sweet spot. Not too fast, or you'll burn out. Not too slow, or you'll drop out.

In the grace race, our code of conduct is the Bible, with all its instructions that tell us how to please God and enjoy Jesus. We have new values, a new purpose, a new direction and a new finish line. We are told where to get spiritual nourishment. We are warned of trip hazards like sin snares or relying on our own efforts or on religious rules.

We have everything we need to run in the sweet spot. What could possibly go wrong?

Falling from Grace

Soon after Oscar received his race acceptance, he took on a different demeanour. He had started his training well but had then injured his leg, proving he was not up to a marathon. With his hands resting on his waist, his eyes travelled to his dirty trainers. The negative thoughts came thick and fast: *I am unfit. I have no experience. I'm not good enough. This was such a stupid idea!*

Oscar's face lost his smile, and his head was down. On a camera, you would see a defeated man gripping crumpled paper.

What changed? Instead of focusing on his gifted acceptance, he looked *in* and *down*, and the results weren't pretty! He had fallen from grace.

In our culture, the phrase "fallen from grace" is often used when someone gets caught doing something awful.

But the phrase is used differently in the Bible. When Paul accused the Galatians of falling from grace (Galatians 5:4), it was because they had forgotten that Jesus had paid for their sin, and they were bankrupting themselves trying to prove that *they* could pay. Someone had persuaded them that Jesus wasn't enough to save them, and that they also needed religious rituals like circumcision. The Galatians gave up freedom and returned to the weak and miserable strategies of the rat race.

"You were running a good race," Paul says in frustration (v 7). "Who cut in on you to keep you from obeying the truth?"

The Galatians were living as if Jesus had died for nothing. If you trust in anybody or anything apart from Jesus in your quest for a "not guilty" verdict, Paul would say you've fallen from grace and returned to being wrapped up in yourself.

This is what happens, isn't it? We get saved and start running, lost in wonder, love and praise. But soon a hurdle gets in our way. It might be failure or rejection. Perhaps it's an unexpected life event like ill health, redundancy or divorce. Or we simply have a bad day.

Whatever the trial, it'll arouse painful feelings such as self-doubt, anxiety or jealousy, accompanied by difficult thoughts like "Why me? Can God be trusted? What's the point?"

The enemy of our soul delights to use this to trigger rat-race flashbacks and drive us into life-limiting or sinful behaviours.

Back to the Rat Race

Consider this everyday example. Someone arrives at the church meeting. They are attractive and well dressed and have a fancy job title. Painful feelings of insecurity assault you, bringing thoughts like these:

"I'm not good enough."

"If these Christians knew how inadequate I am..."

"I have to prove God was right to accept me."

In this trial, the Holy Spirit longs for you to remember that your case is finished. If you do, you'll hold your head high and shake the person's hand. But if you forget grace, you'll withdraw into your inner courtroom, tempted to believe the above thoughts and feelings.

If Jesus isn't your defence, only rat-race strategies are available—self-promotion or self-protection.

SELF-PROMOTION

- Boasting to make sure everyone knows I'm not stupid
- Using big words in prayer to show my intelligence
- Volunteering for every rota to prove my worth
- Self-justifying
- Competing
- Lying about my achievements
- Lying about others to make myself look better
- Trying to make my work, home or leisure life sound more impressive

SELF-PROTECTION

- Withdrawing from the discussion and not attending the next meeting because "I have nothing to bring"
- Belittling others to show who is the greatest
- Avoiding public prayer in case I sound stupid

- Being defensive
- Blaming others for deliberately making me feel like this
- Ruminating on past guilt or thinking of myself as the victim
- Going home and eating or playing video games just to make myself feel better

What about you? How will you behave towards that new person if you believe you are lesser than them or not good enough? Or if you blame them for your discomfort? How likely are you to contribute to the meeting, and what contributions will you make? What will you do when you get home?

Or perhaps it's a different scenario that would trigger painful or anxious thoughts. As you imagine it, consider: What thoughts and feelings grab your attention? When you're thinking those thoughts, do you see rat-race or grace-race conduct? What does it look like on a camera? Will your actions be in keeping with the grace-race code of conduct?

This process is so annoyingly fast and automatic. Feelings of hurt, panic and shame are so quickly triggered. Then we get lost in negative thoughts. Before we realise it, we have forgotten Jesus, ignored his gift wrap and defaulted to ratty behaviour! We're still saved—nothing can take that away—but we're not living like it.

In that place, all we have are the fig leaves of self. Self-promotion will increase the risk of burnout. It's exhausting. Self-protection will leave you sad and lonely and liable to drop out. Which will you be most vulnerable to? Satan is happy with either because both will rob you of joy. Outside of grace, you'll feel uncertain about your salvation. You'll stop enjoying your run and avoid connecting to your fellow runners. Self-preoccupation is slavery, and it results in a sense of burden, self-doubt and shame. When we fall from grace, it shows on the outside.

But there's another way! The Holy Spirit's purpose is to transform your inner life by pointing you to Jesus and away from yourself. If you let him do so, you'll run with your head held high, knowing your verdict is decided and your case is finished. Then others will be able to see what grace and mercy look like on a camera.

Pause for a Look in God's Mirror

Still yourself before God. Take notice of a few breaths. Listen to what you can hear.

Notice any thoughts and feelings arising from what you have read.

Prayerfully read Galatians 5:1-8.

Do you feel weighed down by guilt and shame? What drives you back into your inner courtroom even though your case is finished?

Ask the Spirit to reveal what stops you believing God's grace when you struggle. Is it pride—"Surely my good works are worth something"? Is it shame—"I don't deserve grace"?

With every hard thought or painful feeling, we can choose what clothes to wear and who to believe.

Now read John 3:17.

Jesus didn't come to condemn you. You were already condemned by your sin. Jesus came as your friend to set you free from guilt, shame and fear of exposure. Understanding that but consistently returning to the inner courtroom is like collecting a prescription but not taking the pills!

Be a grace-race participant. Wrapped in Jesus, with the Holy Spirit inside of you, there is no hurt so deep it can't be healed. No brokenness that can't be restored. No rat-race desire you can't be free from. RUN!

Song to sing: *Good and Gracious King* by CityAlight

CHAPTER 4

OUR CODE OF CONDUCT

A few years ago, I stopped at a junction, unlike the lady in the Range Rover who crashed into the back of my car at full speed. The accident injured my back and neck, putting me in constant pain and causing me to struggle to move my upper body. I tried everything, but nothing worked. In the end, I submitted my body to a physiotherapist. Her expert hands straightened me out, and my flexibility instantly improved. However, she said that in order to get the complete, pain-free recovery I craved, I needed to follow her guidelines and stay in touch.

Each day, I got up, retrieved her handout and attempted the prescribed stretches. When I got stuck, I called her for encouragement and further clarity. If she hadn't heard from me, she would pursue me to find out how I was doing.

Often, I didn't want to do my exercises. Sometimes, it hurt me to do so. Frequently, I had a million easier things to do. I persisted for three reasons. I was so grateful for her healing intervention. I believed that her intentions were good and that following her rules would enable me to thrive. Finally, I enjoyed the supportive relationship, and eventually we became friends.

At first, the exercises felt unnatural, but each day I trusted my physiotherapist's instructions, the pain lessened and movement became easier. As a consequence, life became enjoyable again.

Straightening Out

Augustine of Hippo rightly pointed out that sin curves us in on ourselves. Before we come to Jesus, we are naturally bent over and inward-looking, making our lives painful and our freedom limited. It's as if we have spiritually crumbling spines. But Jesus can heal us. If we let him, he'll be our spiritual physiotherapist, working within us to change our heart posture so we can look upward and outward, just as he did.

Much like my physiotherapist, Jesus already "began a good work" within us when he took our sins at the cross (Philippians 1:6). And much like my physiotherapist, he is also committed to finishing our transformation. One day he will glorify us, but the process can start now. God gifts us with everything we need to change and invites us to partner with him in the process of becoming straightened out.

Just as with our physical bodies, our spiritual birth is instant, but our growth to maturity is a long and slow process! To grow up and enjoy the full life we're promised, we need to partner with God by doing what he says in his word. The commandments and instructions in Scripture are our expert's advice sheet.

Having enjoyed the initial healing and new freedom I got

from the physio treatment, I could have thrown away my therapist's advice sheet. I could have thought, "What has my body got to do with her? How dare she tell me what to do? I'm the expert in my own life." When she pursued me, I could have ignored her. When I was stuck, I could have blamed her or given up. But if I had ignored her guidelines for restoration, my neck would have remained painful and immobile. I would no longer be able to look up or out. How sad would that be?

My physiotherapist didn't invest in my healing so that I could stay in bed. She resolved my injury so that I could live again—so I could comfortably sit in church and in the cinema and at work, and so I could stand in queues and complete long walks with friends and family. She gave me the opportunity to live a full life.

God didn't save us so we could stay in bed, smiling about grace and freedom. He healed us so we could live lives worthy of our salvation (Ephesians 1:4), to be his trophies of grace in a hurting world (Ephesians 2:7-9), to do the good works prepared for us (Ephesians 2:10) and to testify to our expert healer.

Here is how Paul sums this up in Galatians 5:25:

> *Since we live by the Spirit, let us keep in step with the Spirit.*

The Holy Spirit lives in every believer, reminding us of Jesus' words and helping us to obey. But we still need to choose to co-operate with the Spirit's work. To live out the gospel of grace in every detail of our lives, we need to look carefully at our expert's advice sheet!

The Rules of the Grace Race

What six-letter word fits the gap in all of these sentences?

People who know their ...... have better relationships.

People who know their ...... enjoy improved mental and physical fitness.

People who know their ...... are better at managing stress.

People who know their ...... are less likely to burn out.

This is the first question I ask in my training programmes. The missing word is "values". Values are the qualities a person wants to show in their behaviour, even when no one is looking. They're like a personal code of conduct.

The relevant research shows that there are many physical and psychological benefits to knowing and showing your values. So, as a psychologist, I have helped thousands of people to identify the values that they want to guide their actions.

In our Western culture, there is no longer a universally agreed code of conduct—which is why I ask non-Christian clients to identify their *own* values. Yet interestingly, I find that the same themes come up again and again. The most popular values include patience, love, kindness, honesty, faithfulness, forgiveness, generosity, compassion and self-control. It shouldn't surprise us that these are God's values, revealed in the Bible! We have been made in God's image to reflect his qualities, and, despite the distortion of sin, God's values are etched on every human heart.

As Christians, we don't need to identify our own values, because God's values have been gifted to us within the

Scriptures. We can be sure that these are the values that will take us back to our spiritual sweet spot—helping us look *up* to God and *out* to others.

All Scripture is useful for showing us how to live using God's code of conduct, but to keep things simple, here is just one well-known verse containing nine key values:

> *But the fruit of the Spirit is love, joy, peace, forbearance, kindness, goodness, faithfulness, gentleness and self-control. (Galatians 5:22-23)*

You might like to copy out this list in your own writing. Add any other biblical values that come to mind. Then take a moment to read what you've written. Maybe you'd like to display it or keep it in the front of your Bible. These are God's values, and getting to know them is the first step to using them.

But getting to know them isn't enough on its own. Knowing God's values but not living by them is like refusing to obey the expert's recommendations but constantly complaining of a stiff neck!

Moving Towards God's Values

Russ Harris is one of my favourite ACT practitioners. He has published a YouTube video called "The Choice Point". It's just a few minutes long and well worth watching. The video introduces two useful but simple concepts. Firstly, the choice point, and secondly, TOWARDS and AWAY actions.

Let's start with the choice point.

Every day we complete many actions and say many words. I get up, get washed, eat, say good morning, grab a take-out coffee, write reports, make calls, walk past people, and so on. Each day offers many moments when we choose one action over another—a choice point.

Sometimes, the choice is big and important: shall I change my job or not? But mostly the choices are small: shall I drink tea or coffee, eat a biscuit or go without? Often, though not always, we are choosing either to walk with the Spirit and remember God's values or to be driven by our sinful hearts into doing wrong.

Russ Harris uses the term "a TOWARDS move" to describe an action that is in line with your values. An action that is in the opposite direction to your values he calls "an AWAY move". I find this simple idea useful.

For the purposes of this book, I am going to define a TOWARDS action as doing something that will take you closer to God's values. I am going to define an AWAY move as an action that will take you away from God's values. With every choice point, however small the choice, I can choose to listen to the Spirit or to let my sinful flesh dominate.

My husband just walked in. I feel irritated at being disturbed. Will I sigh and roll my eyes, or will I smile? When he asks me later what I bought at the shops, will I tell the truth or pretend I spent less than I did? TOWARDS God's values or AWAY? More like Jesus or more like my sinful self?

Each action is changing you in one direction or the other. This is true physically: if I do my exercises, I'll stay flexible, whereas if I don't, I'll get stiff. But it's also true of our inner lives. Each choice adds up, and gradually we change. The more TOWARDS actions you choose, the more able you will be to look up and out; you'll become more like Jesus and less self-focused.

We can get better at walking in step with the Spirit using God's values by intentionally planning TOWARDS moves. At the end of the chapter, I will show you three exercises to help you with this.

When an AWAY Move Looks Like a TOWARDS Move

God's values need to be shown in our actions, but we don't want to end up like the religious people Jesus criticised, doing right behaviours for the wrong reasons. The Pharisees showed an outward veneer of doing good without inner heart change. We mustn't confuse rule-obedience with trust and growth in Jesus through the Spirit's power.

Imagine a dog racing past your window. Is that dog running TOWARDS food or AWAY from a wild animal?

Who knows?!

The dog will know. Running towards food feels exciting and easy. It's very different to the fear and urgency of fleeing from an enemy. But to an outside observer, it's difficult to tell which the dog is experiencing.

When you look at me serving or praying, you can't know if I'm making a TOWARDS or an AWAY move. I could be seeking to please God—a TOWARDS move. Alternatively, I could be people-pleasing to run from negative feelings—an AWAY move.

Remember how we talked about what our inner thoughts would look like on CCTV—how they cause us to act? On a camera, TOWARDS actions can look the same as AWAY actions. They can even look the same to the person doing them!

This matters. Actions that look good but are actually driven by a desire for affirmation or to escape difficult feelings will be thirsty behaviours. Over time, they'll demand more from you. They'll exhaust you and steal your peace, assurance and joy.

We need to use God's values as disciples, not Pharisees. Disciples are Jesus-satisfied. Pharisees are self-satisfied. We need to live out God's values with grateful hearts and heads held high *because* we're accepted and loved, not *in order to* gain acceptance and love from God or others. Then we'll want to show God's values to prove Jesus worthy and not ourselves.

So how do we know whether we're using God's values with the right motives? We'll learn to understand this as we understand better what's going on in our inner selves. This will be addressed in Part 2.

Three Exercises to Move Towards God's Values

1. IDENTIFYING TOWARDS MOVES

First, we're going to look back and spot TOWARDS moves we have made in the past. Start by choosing one of God's values. I am going to choose honesty.

Can you think of any examples from the last week when you have shown your chosen value in your words or actions? Here are my honesty examples:

- When my husband asked me how much my dress cost, I told the truth.

- When the church women's worker asked if I was okay, I admitted I was struggling.
- When a friend asked for guidance about teaching within church, I gently told the truth. I didn't feel that teaching was his gift.

Now choose a second value. Can you think of any examples from the last few weeks when you have shown this chosen value in your words or actions?

2. PLANNING TOWARDS MOVES

Now we're going to use God's values to plan some future TOWARDS actions. The size of the action doesn't matter. Start small but be as specific as you can. This makes it more noticeable when the choice point comes.

Here are my examples for the value of thankfulness:

- When I buy my daily sandwich, I'll give eye contact to the barista and say an intentional thank you.
- On Wednesday morning, before I start my work, I'll send someone a text expressing gratitude for something I appreciate.
- I will end each day by writing down the individual blessings I've enjoyed. Then, on Saturday evening, I'll read and meditate for five minutes on the blessings of the week.

Now it's your turn! Choose a value and write down some actions.

What was it like for you to do those two exercises? Did you notice any thoughts and feelings?

Perhaps, as you reflect on your behaviour, there's obvious

evidence of the Spirit's work in your life. That's a good thing! Thank God that his values are bearing good fruit in your life. Be encouraged and keep going.

Maybe you're more like me. Perhaps you felt self-doubt, guilt, anxiety or thoughts of failure. Remember that Jesus has finished the race on your behalf.

It is helpful to keep a record of your planned actions in a notebook or on your phone. Make a note of any difficult thoughts and feelings that arise. We hurt where we care, so it's impossible to do anything important without some inner turbulence.

3. DEVELOPING A CODE OF CONDUCT

Finally, let's plan how we might intentionally use God's values over a longer time period. We might think about this as our grace-race code of conduct. If you were using God's values as a constant guide to your behaviour, what would that look like on a camera over the next three months?

Here are a few reflection questions to use before you plan. You might find it helpful to discuss these with a friend.

If I intentionally use God's values to guide my life...

- how would it change the way I use my time? What might I do less of or stop doing? What might I start doing?
- what difference would it make to the way I speak at home or at work? What might I say more? What might I stop saying?
- how might it change my responses when I feel pressured, hurt or irritated?

- how might I make better use of the gifts and resources God has given me?
- what might I stop or start watching or listening to?
- how might my messages and emails reflect God's image?
- how might my online presence change?
- how might my behaviour impact those around me?

Now choose some TOWARDS actions or words that will reflect God's values over the next day, week, month, and three months. Make your chosen moves as specific as you can—you might include the time, place and person involved. This isn't about changing everything in your life but about choosing some specific actions that you can realistically make. Write down your chosen moves. This is your personal grace-race code of conduct!

Here are a few examples from my own. You'll see that I've added in brackets some of the sinful or unhelpful thoughts, feelings and desires that have the potential to drive me AWAY from God's values. That's because noticing these inner saboteurs is the first step to inner change. We'll talk more about that in the next few chapters.

Value 1: Faithfulness. Specifically, I want to be faithful to God and to God's people.

- *Over the next 24 hours:* I'll call the friend who missed church.
- *Over the next week:* Before I go to sleep, I'll read a few verses from my Bible and listen to a worship song (even if that leaves me with no time to scroll on my phone). I'll attend our church's outreach cafe for an hour.
- *Over the next month:* I'll stay for coffee at church on at

least two Sundays rather than rush home (even if I'd rather not). I'll offer to do a reading in church (even though I'll experience anxiety).

- *Over the next three months:* I'll attend the mid-week meeting at least once a month.

Value 2: Self-control.

- *Over the next 24 hours:* I will forgo my take-out coffee and give the money to charity.
- *Over the next week:* I'll eat a piece of fruit and drink a bottle of water daily to improve my health and ability to serve.
- *Over the next month:* I'll leave my phone out of my bedroom on weekdays to avoid doom-scrolling so I can get up earlier, pray and be on time (even though it's soothing to scroll). I will be on time for my morning meetings. When I am tempted to join in with office gossip, I'll change the subject.
- *Over the next three months:* I'll go for a walk at least once a week to calm my nervous system and improve my fitness so I'm less tired.

Pause for a Look in God's Mirror

Still yourself before God. Take notice of a few breaths.

How many of God's values can you recall without referring to your list? We need to know God's values and show God's values. Pray for the Spirit to point out your choice points in the coming weeks. Initially, you'll spot them after the choice point opportunity has gone. Gradually, if you let him, the Spirit will make you more sensitive in the moment.

Prayerfully read Romans 12:1-3.

As you do your chosen TOWARDS moves, notice what it feels like. Notice the thoughts that get in the way. Sometimes it will feel hard. Going God's way isn't always easy, but it's worth it. Ask the Spirit to energise you into TOWARDS actions despite any uncomfortable or wrong thoughts and feelings.

The grace race has a slow and steady pace. You'll trip and fail—we all do. When you notice AWAY moves, the accuser will dangle your flimsy fig leaves, encouraging you to cover yourself with something that is not Christ. Stop. Feel the softness of your race shirt. Notice that you've taken an AWAY move. Apply the soothing ointment of grace and get up. No need to rush. When you're ready—run!

Before you put this book down, what is the next right thing you can do or say?

Song to sing: *His Glory and My Good* by CityAlight

PART TWO

THORNS THAT ENTANGLE

I do a lot of walking along narrow paths. On one occasion, something discarded in the hedge distracted me. As I bent down to investigate, a thorny branch hooked itself into my coat. I was furious. Impatiently I yanked my jacket in an attempt to gain freedom, but as I did so, a second branch got me! Before I knew it, I was fully entangled. I'd lost my balance and fallen backwards, and I couldn't move. I felt helpless and hopeless.

In this situation, how much control did I have over my arms and legs? None! I was fully entangled and unable to get back on the path, let alone make progress towards my destination.

Simple thoughts and fleeting feelings have the same potential as a thorny branch to snag us. If we don't know how to disentangle from that initial thought, image, memory, emotion or desire, we'll soon be stuck within the dense thorn bush of a frantic mind, heart-wrenching emotions and overwhelming desires. Then we will be unable to move towards God's values. We will be likely to fall into sinful behaviour (doing wrong) or fall from grace (trying to justify ourselves instead of leaning on Christ). We end up looking in and down instead of up and out.

In the next four chapters, we are going to learn skills from psychology that will help us pay better attention to what is going on inside us so that we get snagged less often. We'll also move on to disentangling skills so that when we do get snagged, we can quickly notice and unhook. Gradually we'll learn to run without falling, whatever our distressed hearts are thinking, feeling or wanting.

The point here is not to focus on the question of what is sinful and what is just unhelpful, nor is it to think about whose fault something is. It's about moving forward—moving towards Jesus. Or as Hebrews puts it...

> *Let us throw off everything that hinders and the sin that so easily entangles. And let us run with perseverance the race marked out for us, fixing our eyes on Jesus, the pioneer and perfecter of faith. (Hebrews 12:1-2)*

Don't forget that each chapter builds on the skills learned in the previous one. So take your time. Don't be tempted to go too fast!

CHAPTER 5

PAYING ATTENTION

This morning, I walked past a man tugging his toddler away from a ladybird. When the child saw me looking, he pointed to his brightly coloured boots. "New ones," he said with a proud grin.

This toddler was full of joy and curiosity, enjoying the pleasures of that moment. He wasn't worrying that I would judge his clothes or think badly of him. He wasn't travelling back in his mind to regret his behaviour at preschool, or worrying that no one would play with him tomorrow.

This is a superpower that most adults have lost: paying attention to what is happening in the moment. That little boy was really there, experiencing life through his senses. He was looking, listening, smelling and touching. He was giving all his attention to the present—really noticing what was going on.

As we mature, paying childlike attention becomes increasingly difficult because we get easily entangled by what's going on inside of us and lose connection with what's going on outside of us. This stops us relating well to God and others and stops us enjoying the life we've been gifted.

The problem is that it happens so fast. One minute you're paying good attention to the road as you drive to church, looking forward to the service, feeling grateful for family. Then a car pulls out without indicating. Before you realise it, you're ruminating and raging. Then a feeling of anxiety grabs your attention. You start worrying, running through your problems in your mind, telling yourself about everything that's going to go wrong today. As you finally rush late into church and take your seat, you're grouchy with your children and you pretend you haven't seen the new person sitting on their own. You left the house running with gusto, but now you're entangled, face down in a thorny bush!

When your body is in one place but your mind is somewhere else, psychologists call it "autopilot". It's as if we have a mental time machine that travels us into the past to revisit failure and disappointment, arousing feelings of regret and guilt, or that transports us to our imagined future, creating disproportionate fear and worry. On autopilot, we lose connection with what we can see, hear, touch, taste and smell—it's the opposite to paying attention to what's going on in the here and now. This matters because on autopilot we take the easy route, and often (though not always) the easy route is the sinful route.

In 1 Corinthians 3, Paul is disappointed with the behaviour of the Christians at Corinth. He lists sinful behaviours like jealousy and quarrelling, and accuses his readers of acting like "mere humans" (v 3). In older translations, "mere humans" is translated as "carnal". This means being driven by bodily urges, having lost control of your own actions. In other words, these Christians are on autopilot. Their flesh has taken the steering wheel, driving them away from God's values, while the wisdom that comes from Christ is tied up on the back seat.

Come to Your Senses

The opposite of autopilot is paying attention, and there is plenty of research to confirm that doing this is beneficial. When you simply pause to pay attention—using your senses, focusing on what you can see, hear, feel, taste and touch—it pulls you out of autopilot and gets you on a better track. It helps you stay calm and ultimately improves your health, relationships and mental performance. I have experienced this to be true, and I teach my clients to pay better attention by using their five senses.

Psychologists sometimes refer to these skills as grounding techniques. Tuning in to your senses—what you can hear, see, smell, touch or taste—is a useful way of regaining emotional stability in moments of overwhelm. Grounding yourself might be as simple as listening to the birds before getting in your car, or noticing something new in your environment.

However, using your senses is not simply about slowing down in a moment of anxiety.

The phrase "come to your senses" is used several times in Scripture (1 Corinthians 15:34; 2 Timothy 2:26; Luke 15:17). There are other, similar phrases too: be sober-minded, be careful, wake up, stay alert and be on your guard. These are all commands to come off autopilot in order to change direction, to stop sinning and instead to walk in step with the Spirit: to stop moving AWAY and instead move TOWARDS God's values. As Paul puts it...

> *Be very careful, then, how you live—not as unwise but as wise, making the most of every opportunity, because the days are evil. Therefore, do not be foolish, but understand what the Lord's will is. (Ephesians 5:15-17)*

At church the other day, I saw a lady in tears and heard her say, "I hope he comes to his senses." Her son had left his wife and two children.

Why did the mother long for her son to come to his senses? Was it so that he could detach from his inner world or enjoy inner peace and healing?

No!

She wanted him to see the heartbreak he was creating for others. She wanted him to listen to his conscience and restore his family. In other words, she wanted him to come to his senses in order to *change*. It wasn't just about coming out of autopilot and having a more tranquil mind. It was about paying attention to what is really true and important.

Coming to your senses means disconnecting from your inside distractions to reconnect with reality so that you can do what's right.

With all that in mind, let's learn the skills needed to pay better attention!

The Mind Has Two Gears

Not many people realise that the human brain has been designed with two gears: thinking and sensing.

Thinking gear is dominated by language and enables us to solve problems and achieve goals. If you didn't have thinking gear, you couldn't read or understand your Bible, let alone remember it or do what it says. Without our thinking abilities, we would be lost! However, the rat race drags us into thinking gear inappropriately and far too often. Rather than solving problems that are within our control, we use thinking to worry and ruminate on things we can't do anything about. Rather than using our mental time machine to recall relevant information and make effective plans, we dredge up grudges and catastrophise about the future.

The other gear is sensing. We've been placed in an amazing world and given our senses to relax and enjoy it. Our ability to touch, taste, see, hear and smell enhances our relationships and most of our experiences. Our senses keep us safe and enable us to flourish according to our design.

Pause for a moment. Notice that you're breathing and pay attention to a few breaths. Now listen for two things you can hear, and see if you can smell anything. You've switched from thinking gear to sensing gear. Now, work out what time you need to next leave the house. You've returned to thinking gear.

Both gears are useful, but if we live permanently in the wrong gear, we'll burn out, miss out or opt out. We need to pay attention and intentionally switch gear when necessary.

When I'm looking out of the window at the birds instead of doing my work, I'm in sensing gear when I need to be thinking. When I'm ruminating about my work on a leisure walk with my family, I'm using thinking gear unhelpfully.

I would encourage you to pause for a few seconds at intervals in the day. Set an alarm to remind yourself. Ask yourself: am I in thinking gear or sensing gear? Which is most helpful for this situation?

How to Change Gears

If you're in thinking gear when you should be in sensing gear, what do you do? Well, with practice, we can use our body and our five senses as a mental clutch to change gear. Here are some simple exercises you can add in to your day to get better at paying careful attention by using your senses.

- When completing a routine activity like showering, eating or driving, notice what you can see, taste, smell, touch and feel.
- Pause and take notice of five breaths. Notice which parts of your body move as you breathe in and out. Notice the sensations in your body. Where do you feel them?
- Push your feet into the floor and notice what it feels like.
- Notice what changes as you move from an inside environment to outside.
- When waiting, resist your phone. What can you see, hear, taste and smell?
- Pay attention to those you love. Give them eye contact. Notice the tiny details as they smile and talk.

Each time you use the ideas above to come to your senses, ask yourself...

- What am I doing in this moment?
- Is my behaviour in line with what God wants from me?
- Is there a relationship opportunity here?
- Am I missing the joy or blessing that is available in this moment?
- What can I thank God for in this moment, however hard it is?

As you take small pauses to come to your senses, you'll get better at catching yourself at the choice points and adjusting your behaviour before you stumble. Recently, my husband and I were walking and talking about a stressful situation when we realised we were becoming a little too irritated with each other. Taking a moment to pause and come to our senses, we noticed the beauty of our surroundings, the smell of a nearby farm and the quietness of the countryside. Having done that, we continued our walk with gratitude and a kinder attitude towards each other.

Here is another skill that will help. I devised the STOMP technique for my secular practice to help people pay better attention, but I've adapted it for this book. The beginning is familiar, as we've been doing it in mirror moments.

- S: *Still yourself before God.* Simply stop what you're doing and remember that God is God and you are not.
- T: *Take notice of a few breaths.* You are not trying to relax or change your breathing but just to notice you are breathing and where you can feel it. Rejoice that you are fearfully and wonderfully made.

- O: *Observe your inner life.* Is your mind busy or calm? If busy, what thoughts are snagging you? Consider what you are feeling. Start with physical feelings: are you tired, hot, hungry, thirsty? Then ask what you are feeling emotionally. Are you calm, sad, anxious, frustrated? Where in your body do you notice these feelings?
- M: *Move any part of your body.* Notice that you still have control of your actions despite your inner world. Open your mouth. Nod your head. Push your hands together or lift them high. Stand up and walk.
- P: *Present yourself as a living sacrifice* (Romans 12:1). What and who is important right now? What are you supposed to be doing? What is the smallest action you could take to move closer to God or others? Come to your senses and get on with it.

When you're well practised, you'll find that this technique is helpful to use in moments of upset, panic or anger. Sometimes feeling calmer will be the fortunate side effect of a STOMP, but don't be mistaken: the purpose is not to get rid of your feelings but to notice and disentangle from them in order to make TOWARDS moves.

I would encourage you to practise a STOMP at least four times a day to begin with. (Try pairing it with a routine activity like washing your hands, boiling water or putting on your shoes.) STOMPing is a skill, and like any skill, it will take practice to produce change.

Unless you've grasped and practised the idea when calm, it won't be helpful when you feel overwhelmed.

Persevering

There is brain-scan evidence to prove that practising these skills changes your brain. After about three months, you should find it easier to pay attention and switch gear. Often people notice that they feel calmer and enjoy life more.

But there is a downside to paying better attention: you'll notice that your inner life is messier than you hoped! For many, this is troubling, which is why they prefer autopilot. Running about like a headless chicken, repeating behaviours that are comfortable, feels easier than facing the mess inside.

If that's you, then you are right: you do have an inner mess. For all of us, there are things in our heart and in our past that we don't like. This is why Jesus had to die. Remember that because of him, you are a *glorious* mess! The Holy Spirit is straightening you out. He is gentle and won't push you beyond the awareness you can bear. He is committed to changing your heart posture and completing your restoration.

STOMP back to the Father. Feel his compassion in success and failure. Consider if it would be helpful to share your inner mess with others. Healing and freedom come from sharing our pain and acknowledging that while we're all different, there is no one who doesn't have an inner mess.

Pause for a Look in God's Mirror

Come to your senses. What can you hear, see, taste and smell?

Prayerfully read Matthew 26:40-41 and Galatians 6:8-10.

As Christians, we need to come to our senses, or we'll drift, backslide and get trapped in cycles of sin. Ask God to increase your awareness so that you can do his will, not yours—for his glory and your good.

An easy way to learn is to teach others. Can you teach a STOMP to someone? It is a great way to anchor yourself in the tsunami of thoughts and feelings.

Song to sing: *Christ Is Mine Forevermore* by CityAlight

CHAPTER 6

SUBCONSCIOUS SABOTEURS

Home group is at Rob and Karen's. They are relaxed hosts with a comfortable home littered with abandoned toys. Karen opens in prayer and effortlessly reads the Bible passage. Rob explains the passage, giving great examples.

Priya, Marsha, Darron and Martin echo the final amen. Karen and Rob make the coffee and invite people to stay for fellowship. Darron feels encouraged and grateful. But... Marsha feels jealous and enraged. Martin feels sad, rejected and a failure. Priya feels insecure and anxious.

How on earth can four people respond so differently to the same situation?

During home group, something about Karen's youthful ways and the children's toys triggered Marsha's old feelings about being childless and unwanted—not good enough. Marsha's mind offers these thoughts to solve her feelings:

- *Everyone likes Karen more than me. Who does she think she is? She's got no life experience.*
- *If only I were still young and attractive. If only I had children.*

How does this show on a camera? Marsha ignores Karen during coffee time, speaking loudly to the others about her success at work. On her way home, she books a hair appointment and manicure.

During home group, something about Rob's physical presence triggers Martin's old feelings about being short and unmanly—not good enough. Martin's mind offers these thoughts to solve his feelings:

- *Rob is better at everything. Why do I even bother?*
- *No one asked how I was. Everyone thinks I'm useless. No one wants to talk to me.*

How does this look on a camera? Martin rushes away before coffee. He ruminates on his failings on the drive home. He feels so crushed that he takes a day off work, leaving his colleagues overstretched. He feels isolated and low, so he doesn't make it to church on Sunday.

During home group, something about Karen and Rob's effortless facilitation triggers Priya's old feelings of being intellectually inadequate—not good enough. Priya's mind offers these thoughts to solve her feelings:

- *At least Rob got caught out on some tricky questions. He's not as great as he thinks.*
- *I won't get caught out when I take the study next week. I'll show them who is the mature Christian.*

How does this look on a camera? Priya is quiet during coffee time. When she gets home, she cancels a family night out to over-prepare her study. She stays up listening to sermons on that passage. She is tired and irritable with her children.

Yikes. Where did all that come from?

The thoughts, images and memories that arise in our minds, and the emotions and desires that present as feelings in our bodies, are all part of our good design. However, because our minds and bodies are sadly polluted by sin, our thoughts and feelings often function like sneaky thorn branches or race saboteurs. When I'm least expecting it, a sinful or unhelpful thought jumps into my mind, and before I know it, it has taken over.

Some inner saboteurs are conscious. For example, earlier, I noticed a feeling of anxiety about an upcoming meeting. Right now, I have the urge to eat something sweet. But other inner saboteurs arise from our subconscious. These are thoughts, images, beliefs and feelings that we are not aware of, making them harder to catch and manage.

In this chapter, I am going to explain how the subconscious produces subtle feelings in our bodies which change our actions without us even noticing. In chapters 7 and 8 we will deal with the conscious thoughts and feelings.

The Fear Response

When you're in a public place, you'll be unaware of being monitored by CCTV. But if you leave a bag unattended, within minutes, security guards will storm in to save the day. No time for questions. Better safe than sorry.

The nervous system works in much the same way. When we feel vulnerable, powerless, worthless or inadequate, our brains detect those feelings as if they are unattended bags. Adrenalin and cortisol, our chemical security guards, are sent to sort it out. It's called "the fear response" or "fight or flight". People commonly feel agitated, restless, panicked, stressed or intensely emotional. Often, this will produce a need to fidget or escape the situation. This all happens without conscious awareness, so those big feelings can come as a surprise.

If a tree is about to fall on you, the fear response is exactly what you need. You'll get the energy to run. But if unnoticed or arising at an unhelpful moment, the fear response has great potential to drive you to AWAY moves.

Many people have heard of the fear response, but most don't realise how frequently it's triggered and how it impacts our ability to stay in the sweet spot. Those chemical security guards behave like sneaky mind-altering drugs! They change our senses so that we mishear what is said and see neutral faces as angry or frightening. More importantly, they switch off the mind's spam filter so that our inner mess tricks us into believing irrational, paranoid and self-focused thoughts that make God out to be a liar and others our enemy.

- *I'm not safe. I can't trust God to handle this. I need to take control.*
- *This sadness will last for ever. I can't move. The world is against me.*

- *I'm disgusting—only an awful person would do what I just did. God can't love someone like me. I must hide.*
- *I've blown it this time. Nobody else is as bad as me. I'll always fail. It's not worth trying.*

Here's an example: I marched into a meeting with my head held high, feeling calm and competent. Then in walked a lady, younger than me, in a sharp suit with perfect make-up. "Hello," she beamed. "I'm the company psychologist." Before I could blink, my hands shook, and my insides turned to jelly. I felt overwhelmed and restless. I wanted to run or hide under the table.

Something about the presence of the perfectly friendly psychologist had triggered fear. In a state of stress, my mind jumped to faulty conclusions: *I am not up to this. No one likes me. She's out to get me.*

Interestingly, however, a few months later I met that corporate psychologist for coffee. She disclosed that she had also felt threatened and insecure at our first meeting. We became friends. Us flawed humans are a complex lot!

Most of us experience the fear response when we feel vulnerable, inadequate or not good enough. How easily and frequently it happens will depend on the unique combination of your genetics, your early relationships and your life experiences. Our historical emotional wounds are like land mines buried in our bodies, waiting to be triggered—and triggers can be anything: a smell, a sight, a taste, a season, a word, a tone of voice, a personality type, an email, a phone notification, a worrying thought, silence, shouting... or literally anything that reminds the body of a past hurt, even when it's long forgotten by your mind.

Your threat system will be especially sensitive if you've experienced a complex childhood or historical trauma, or if you have a neurodivergent brain. Then, you may even experience a fear response in the face of kindness or physical and emotional intimacy. The good news is that even the most fearful brain can learn to feel more secure when submitted to the healing hands of Jesus.

Pause for a moment when you notice yourself doing a self-protective or self-promoting behaviour (there's a list of these in chapter 4). You may well be responding to a fear response in your body. Ask yourself—what's really the matter? Why has a fear response been triggered?

I often feel the fear response with groups of women or when I feel a failure. I feel it when I'm uncertain, when I'm told what to do, when I'm criticised or when I fear I've made a mistake. However, sometimes I just wake up with that feeling, and often it comes for no apparent reason. Anyone would think my flesh is fighting to call the shots!

Don't Let Those Sneaky Landmines Blow You Up

Ephesians 4:26 reads, "In your anger do not sin". A legitimate extension of that might be: *When flooded with any intense emotion, do not sin.* It's not necessarily the initial feeling that is sinful; it's how we respond to it.

In John 18, Jesus is ambushed by a large group of enemies. Peter is there, and he loves Jesus, so when he sees the soldiers approaching, his fear response kicks in. He can't think. He attacks, cutting off someone's ear. Not long afterwards, when he's challenged by a serving girl in the high priest's courtyard, it happens again: he blurts out that he doesn't know Jesus. In Matthew 26:74, when he's challenged for the third time, Peter is angry and swears at his accuser.

I don't judge Peter—he's much the same as me. But as always, Jesus shows us the better way. Hanging on a cross, he was stripped and publicly humiliated. He remained silent. He looked up, knowing that his Father was good and could be trusted, and he looked out, forgiving those who hung him there. He gave his life without fighting or running away so that we would never again be truly vulnerable or powerless.

As soon as we truly believe in Jesus, our souls are born again. Yet just like Peter, we remain in emotionally scarred bodies, with minds that have been wired with rat-race beliefs. The fear response is automatic—we can't help it—and if we respond to it on autopilot, we will behave sinfully.

But it doesn't have to be this way. In Ephesians 4:22-24, Paul urges the believers "to put off your old self, which is being corrupted by its deceitful desires; to be made new in the attitude of your minds; and to put on the new self, created to be like God in true righteousness and holiness". By the power of the Spirit, we can put on a new self; we can respond with our heads held high, acting in line with our grace-race code of conduct.

Let's consider some tools that will help us understand our fear response and deal with it better.

Fighting, Flighting, Flopping

Pause for a moment and imagine a situation you'd hate to be in: something that fills you with fear or a person you'd rather avoid. Notice carefully where you feel a response in your body—you are probably glimpsing your unique fear response. Where in your body do you feel it? What are the sensations like? How might you describe them to a child?

I feel it in my head and upper chest and throat. My husband experiences rapid swallowing and reflux type feelings. One man I know experiences burping, while another person experiences the symptoms of a cold—he gets a blocked nose and a sore throat. Many aches, pains and stomach problems are the symptoms of not keeping short accounts with our bodily stress responses.

That's what's happening in your body. What about in your mind? What irrational, paranoid or blaming thoughts arise as part of your fear response? What are you vulnerable to believing?

Then, what about outside? What would be seen on a camera?

In your fear response, do you fight (self-promote)—explode, get irritable, become defensive or controlling? Or do you flight (self-protect)—leave the room, numb your pain with food, bury yourself in work?

A third and less well-known stress response is sometimes called "flop". For years, I didn't realise that when my husband seemed switched off, inactive and lethargic, he was actually experiencing flop. In this state, his mind goes blank, his eyes disengage, and he feels numb, exhausted and unable to do anything.

What about you? An essential skill for managing your inner life is to learn what the fear response feels like in your body. Noticing and naming it will bring your rational brain back into play. Say something like "This is my fear response".

We'll be talking more about noticing and naming later on, so don't worry if some of these questions feel too hard to answer at the moment. For now, here's a quick tip. Instead of struggling to get rid of bodily discomfort, view it as an acquaintance you don't much like but who is bringing an important message. We only have difficult feelings when there's something important involved. Emotions show us what we care about and can motivate us to right action when necessary. Not every feeling is godly, and not every feeling is a good guide for our actions—but if we just suppress or ignore our painful emotions, we miss out on their important communications.

Hacking Your Fear Response

The problem is that we often come to our senses too late. The feelings are physical. Receiving reassurance from others, quoting Bible verses and self-talk will often fail, because these things are targeting the mind when the reaction is in the body—it's like disciplining the wrong child! Instead we need to target the body.

The easiest solution is simply to stop and wait. If you're with others, tell them you need a few moments' breathing space. Blow out gently, as if you're extinguishing birthday candles. Give yourself a few minutes, and you'll find that the intensity of your bodily discomfort will quickly pass.

Or try one or two of these hacks to trick your nervous system out of fight and flight:

- Yawn or smile
- Splash your face with cold water
- Go outside
- Sing aloud
- Move your body

Nervous-System Hygiene

I routinely see my dental hygienist. I don't enjoy going, but it prevents the build-up of decay and the resulting painful toothache.

If oral hygiene is important, nervous-system hygiene is vital. How successful we are at managing distress in the moment is mostly to do with how we spend the rest of our time. It is possible to dampen your threat response by being proactive about your "nervous-system hygiene".

Below is a list of ten Cs which have been well researched as activities that have a positive impact on the nervous system. They are all part of God's good design for human flourishing. Consider the list and do what you were designed for! When you do, life should start to feel more enjoyable and meaningful, and you will be better able to manage stressful situations when they come.

- *Choose God.* Start the day with God's mirror, the Bible. Look up!
- *Church commitment.* Go every week. You can't be honest with strangers. Going routinely makes it easy to receive support when you're hurting.
- *Connection with others,* especially God's people. The nervous system is soothed by eye contact, smiles and touch.

- *Creativity.* We are designed to create. Creative pursuits such as art, music, reading or craft will enable you to come to your senses and live as you were designed.
- *Creation enjoyment and care.* Being outside in nature and with animals is soothing.
- *Cardio.* We were created to move! Any movement, however small, helps. Regular exercise is as effective as medication for mild to moderate depression and anxiety.
- *Chill.* All work and no play makes Jack a dull boy... but also a depressed, lonely, tired and sporadic Christian. Take a Sabbath and set boundaries.
- *Contribute.* Don't be a spectator. What gifts have you been given and how can you use them?
- *Consumables.* Fruit and veg contain the nutrients required by your body and mind. Processed food makes you vulnerable to mental and physical illness. More importantly, what is your mind consuming?
- *Count your blessings.* Gratitude is good for you. The Bible says we should rejoice and give thanks!

Back to Karen and Rob's

If our imaginary friends at Karen and Rob's could notice and better respond to their fear state, how might that change what they each do as they go home?

Marsha would remember she is accepted by God despite being rejected early in life. Instead of blaming Karen, she might recognise Karen's repeated efforts to include her, and feel able to talk about the sadness of her infertility. Karen might respond to this honesty by admitting that she feels exhausted and shouts constantly at her kids. As they become friends, Marsha might realise that she enjoys the chaos of Karen's home more than she enjoys overworking and perfectionism. Sometimes she might babysit to give Karen and Rob a break and help their son with his homework.

Martin might remember that God has made each of us just how he wants us to be, and church is the place where we should be free of unbiblical gender stereotypes. He might enjoy sharing the amazing chocolate brownies he made for coffee time while kindly asking Rob if his job is any less stressful these days. He won't stay too late because he wants to pull his weight at work.

Priya would remember that God has gifted everyone differently and that even though she did not do well at school, she is now an excellent administrator and a blessing to her colleagues. She might feel able to give Rob and Karen some positive feedback about how they led the group and thank them for their hospitality. She could accept that her own study will be less academic and more relational because that's her strength. She might head home for an early night so she can be at her best during family time the next day.

Wow! How different our churches would be if we could be emotionally honest with each other.

Polluted by sin, our bodies are faulty detectors, and our minds hold faulty beliefs. But when we are wrapped up in Jesus, we can talk honestly with our heads held high, even in times of fear. There's no need to self-protect or self-promote because, despite our messy insides, we're more loved and accepted than we can imagine.

Spending time with Jesus, knowing you are fully known yet unconditionally loved, and practising your nervous-system hygiene will enable you to be emotionally honest with others and thus enjoy the easy yoke you were created for.

Pause for a Look in God's Mirror

Still yourself before God. Right now, do you feel calm or fearful?

Take notice of a few breaths.

Prayerfully read Mark 4:35-41.

When the disciples are afraid of the storm raging around them, Jesus says they don't need to be. He is in their boat! They should have faith in him, not themselves. The same is true for our own internal storms.

Sometimes, if you cry out to Jesus in a fear moment, he'll miraculously calm your inner storm. Often, your feelings won't change—but each fear moment is an opportunity to strengthen your faith muscles.

Sometimes, in response to fear, your inner Peter will pounce. Read the end of Peter's story in John 21. Instead of shaming his friend for his epic fail, Jesus prepared breakfast for him and recommissioned him. When you are in a place of regret, respond to yourself with the compassion of your Saviour.

If you're willing, ask the Holy Spirit to help you notice your fear response and the things you do when you feel out of control. Ask him for the courage to be vulnerable with others.

Song to sing: *Rest My Soul* by Tim Timmons

CHAPTER 7

FEELING SABOTEURS

"It made me feel good," a teenager told me after she set fire to the school bin.

It's not just teens who do things because it makes them feel good, is it? The motto of our age is *If it feels good, it is good—do it. If it feels bad, it is bad—don't do it.* We're all guilty of sometimes falling for this secular mantra.

But what does it mean to feel good? Feeling good means I am not experiencing any negative feelings. It often means that I am feeling good about myself and the way my life is; that I am presenting myself well to others so that they believe I am healthy, successful and popular.

When I say something unkind, I fail an exam, I am unwell or my child rebels, I feel sad, angry, upset, anxious, guilty, embarrassed or inadequate. I feel bad (about myself). However, when someone tells me I'm wonderful, when I say a thoughtful prayer or make someone laugh, when I am well and my projects are going well, I feel good (about myself).

That phrase "about myself" is important. Naturally, we feel good when we look good... not when God looks good.

In our church, we sometimes sing the line "Would I gladly be made nothing if Christ would be made more?" If I'm honest, although I want to say yes, my heart says NO! I don't want to be ignored, disrespected and taken for granted, even if that lifts Jesus up.

But caring more about when God looks good than when we look good is actually the solution to our woes! Struggling to positively image ourselves is a losing battle—we can't be good enough, so we end up in cycles of dishonesty and shame. Instead we have to remember that the battle has already been won on our behalf. Jesus died to gift us his self-image, so we can drop the pretence and enjoy reflecting *God's* image. What a relief!

This chapter is about responding rightly to our emotions—the good, the bad and the ugly—so that we can live out God's values whatever we feel. We can't do that by trying harder or faking positive emotions. We *can* do it by worshipping God and getting glimpses of how he feels about us, the world and others. Any change of heart is a work of the Spirit as we gaze at Jesus.

We Hurt Where We Care

We were designed to feel our emotions. In my clinical practice, I often say that "we hurt where we care". To stop hurting, we'd have to stop caring—which would make it impossible to love God or others! Imagine climbing a mountain, hugging a child or meeting a friend without feeling anything. People who avoid their emotions eventually feel nothing—nothing bad but also nothing good. Ultimately they become heartless and insensitive.

So, it's not necessarily bad to feel emotional pain. We hurt where we care—and that's good. However, by nature we care about the wrong things and make even the good things into god things. Sin makes us self-obsessed, which means that too often our emotions are self-centred and not God-centred.

This week, I felt gutted when my local coffee shop was closed but mildly irritated when someone left our church. I felt devastated when I weighed myself but uninterested when a colleague lost her job. Frequently, my emotions show me what I value but not what God values. You can see that as self-obsessed people, our feelings can't be used to guide our actions!

That's also true because emotions are often unpredictable and changeable, and we mostly can't control them. (If I threatened to shoot you if you felt anxious, could you stay alive?) In many ways our emotions are not dissimilar to the average toddler—unpredictable, irrational and hard to control... and would you trust a two-year-old to tell you what to do?

Our emotions are a God-given part of our existence, but they are not always something we should obey. Our feelings are as corrupted by sin as every other part of us. If we just do what feels good, it will lead us away from God.

But the solution isn't just to struggle to get rid of our unwanted emotions.

The Hurt Is Not the Problem

Right now, it's raining. Rain is my least favourite kind of weather. But imagine if I entered into a mental battle with the rain. "Rain, I hate you. It's not fair! Go away! Rain, why are you here? Why me?"

Do you think the rain would hear or obey me? Do you think my mental battle would change the weather? Might my attack make the rain feel worse? Of course not! But would my mental fight make me feel even more unhappy about the rain? Most likely, yes!

Much of the time, the same is true of our emotional weather. When emotions arrive that we don't like, didn't expect or can't explain, we can get drawn into a mental struggle to ignore or get rid of them. But this struggle takes energy and makes the feelings more painful. Instead we need to accept that they are very often just like the British weather—changeable and beyond our control—and then do what's needed *despite* them. (Russ Harris has produced a brief video on YouTube called "The Struggle Switch" to illustrate this point. Worth a watch.)

We also need to remember that while we may not like the rain, growth is impossible without it. Times of struggle are often the seasons that produce the most spiritual growth.

Painful emotions hurt, and nobody likes hurting. The plot twist is that the hurt is not the problem. Just like physical pain, emotional pain is simply there to tell me that something is happening that requires attention. Sometimes a crack in my tooth hurts; other times a crack in my heart hurts. It won't help to ignore it, and it won't help to struggle against it.

So what *should* I do?

John 12 describes the week leading up to Jesus' death.

In verse 27, Jesus expresses how he feels about what's to come:

> *Now my soul is troubled, and what shall I say? "Father, save me from this hour"?*

Here's my paraphrase:

> *I'm feeling distraught, so what am I going to say? Should I ask my Father to rid me of these negative emotions and this scary situation?*

What would I answer if I were Jesus? I would say, "Yes, absolutely, please take these bad feelings. I want to feel good again."

Then I'd add, "Father, it's not fair—why me? I thought you loved me, but you clearly don't. I thought you were good, but you're obviously not. Stop these bad emotions, or I'll use them as an excuse to do my own thing, believe my own lies and take back control of my life."

You're probably braver than me, but Jesus was braver than us all. He said this:

> *No, it was for this very reason I came to this hour. Father, glorify your name! (v 27-28)*

Despite terrible emotional pain, Jesus believed the truth about his Father, himself and others.

Jesus was able to think right, which creates right feelings and right actions. He submitted his wants and comfort to the Father's will and lived out God's values despite feeling terrible.

We need to do the same.

Faulty Beliefs

As a child, I craved love, friendship, acceptance, relationship, compassion and connection. These values were important to me as I'd experienced the pain of rejection. They are God's values too.

But I also held faulty beliefs about myself. I was unlovable. Nice things would make me feel loved. Being attractive was the same as having worth. All of this led me to feelings of jealousy. On one occasion, I actually stole a fancy coat belonging to a pretty friend, and shoved it down a used toilet!

Once grown up, I took my faulty beliefs into my marriage. I believed that if my husband met a better option, he would reject me. The problem was that in my insecure eyes, every woman was a better option! My mind tried hard to solve my jealous and anxious feelings. If I got enough information, surely my feelings would stop. So, I would interrogate my husband. I would seek explanations for my faulty disposition. I would worry, ruminate and catastrophise for hours. Boxes of chocolates and online shops kept me company.

I alternated between being a green-eyed monster who interrogated and controlled and being a shameful mess who loathed that unlovable monster.

But can you see that my emotional pain wasn't the problem? The problem was the faulty beliefs that my pain revealed—and what I did in response. If only I had been emotionally honest with a wise and compassionate person. They could have shared God's opinion of me and shown his compassion. This would have prevented the endless cycles of sin and shame.

Thinking right is the key to feeling right. So, we're going to spend much of the next chapter thinking about how to deal with faulty beliefs. For now, though, let's focus on how to respond better to the feelings themselves.

Don't Go MAD

We naturally try to avoid, get rid of or solve situations that make us feel bad. If there's a bad smell, we walk away. If we're cold, we grab a coat. If there's rubbish, we clear it up. With practical problems that are within our control, this works well. However, it's disastrous when we apply these strategies to get rid of bad feelings.

"Emotional control strategies" is the psychological term. Below, I've grouped the most common strategies under three headings, making the acronym MAD.

You'll see that some MAD behaviours are obviously sinful. Others look better on a camera—maybe even righteous! But my point isn't to focus on what's sinful and what isn't. Whatever you do, MAD behaviours show that you're hurting but don't yet know how to manage your hurt.

- M: *Mind activities.* Overthinking, analysing, worrying, chewing over problems, making to-do lists, thinking about the past or fearing the future.
- A: *Avoidance.* Avoiding activities, people or places to escape difficult feelings. Controlling or restricting people you love.
- D: *Distraction.* Eating, buying, cleaning, gaming, porn, scrolling, films, podcasts. Excessive talking or venting at others. Working, staying busy, drugs and alcohol, relationships, hobbies.

If I watched you on a camera during times of stress, which of these things would I see you doing?

All MAD behaviours leave you thirsty for more. The first time you exercise to rid yourself of emotional pain, half an hour on the treadmill is enough; but soon five hours is insufficient. Cleaning and tidying were a great soother, but now you have little time for anything else. You used to just have a nice glass of wine at the close of the day, but now a bottle isn't enough. These strategies are exhausting, they're distracting and eventually they make you ill! This is not the easy yoke that Jesus wants us to take upon ourselves.

Noticing and Naming

Instead of trying to control our emotions, we need to learn to tolerate them so that we can keep on making TOWARDS moves even when we are feeling bad. Like paying attention, tolerating bad feelings is a skill we need to relearn. It's an easy skill in theory, but it takes practice.

There are three steps. First, noticing.

Do you remember what happened at school when the teacher left the class? The kids went bonkers! Ignored emotions behave like unsupervised kids. They play up, shout louder and even make your body sick. If permanently ignored, they give up and leave you feeling nothing at all.

We need to bring the teacher back into the room. That's what we're doing by simply noticing the sensations showing up in our bodies.

The second step is to name the feelings we've noticed.

It fascinated me to discover that naming our thoughts and feelings ignites the rational part of our brains. By naming the ouch of an emotion, we are inviting the wise, rational part of ourselves to take control again—like the teacher reasserting authority over a rowdy classroom. Our bodies experience greater calm, and our chance of doing right immediately increases.

When you feel something in your body, simply label it aloud or in your mind by saying, "I am noticing a feeling of..." Start with physical sensations—"I am noticing a pang of hunger." Notice what it feels like and where in your body you feel it. Progress to small emotional storms like irritation, impatience and frustration. Then the necessary skills will be well practised when the bigger emotional storms blow in.

If you're unsure what the emotion is, don't worry—we don't always know! Simply say, "I am noticing emotional pain" or "I'm noticing some hard feelings in my chest." Over time you'll get better at knowing. You'll spot the themes and see how different emotions feel different or show up in different parts of your body. It's fascinating!

If it's helpful, you can say, "I've noticed a feeling that's sinful or wrong." In my experience, however, this is mostly not helpful, since we're so polluted by sin that few of our feelings are completely pure. Struggling to identify the wrong ones seems to drive people to inappropriate shame and defeat. Instead simply trust the Spirit to show you the truth as he changes your heart.

Notice how many emotions you can spot each day. Notice any urges towards MAD behaviour. This is not about struggling against or questioning our moods and emotions—simply notice and name them.

Tolerating Feelings

The third step is to tolerate the discomfort of emotional pain. The technique I am about to share with you can be used for emotional or physical pain or unwanted urges or desires. Being curious about how your body responds is the first step to a healthy self-awareness and has been shown to improve resilience and prevent AWAY moves.

If you've been practising your STOMPs, this technique will feel familiar, as it is essentially an extension of the observing "O" within a STOMP. Tolerating distress just requires you to observe for a little longer and to notice more of the detail.

Here's how to practise it.

- Think of a person or situation in the past or present that will arouse a negative emotion like anxiety, jealousy or sadness. Bring to mind the situation—who, what and where—and dwell on it for a moment or two.
- Now notice any sensations in your body and label them. "I am noticing frustration or jealousy or hurt." "I am feeling tightness in my chest."
- Focus on where you can most obviously feel a bodily reaction. If you can't feel anything, notice what numb feels like. Ask yourself these questions:
  - How wide, high and low does the feeling stretch? If I could outline it with a marker pen, what would the shape be?
  - If I gave it a colour, what would it be?

    - Is it a pounding or a still feeling?
    - Is it just on the surface of my body or does it go all the way through me?
    - Is the feeling in just one place, or can I also feel it in other parts of my body?
- Notice any thoughts you have about this feeling. Thoughts like "I can't do this", "It hurts too much", "Why me?".
- Pull back your shoulders. Imagine that the feeling is a trapped bird and needs space to flutter.
- Return your attention to the feeling. It might be bigger; it might be smaller. It doesn't matter, as the purpose of the exercise is to tolerate the pain, not to get rid of it.
- Now move your body. Shake. Nod. Anything to get moving again. What and who is important right now? What's the next right thing you can do?

This is such a strange idea, isn't it? The first time I was introduced to it, I thought it was all a bit weird and silly. But having practised it, I now rave about the benefits.

Watching my feelings initially felt impossible and unnatural. I'm not a visual person, so I'm unable to see emotions in colours or shapes as some people do. However, I can now easily spot a feeling and tolerate it in order to make TOWARDS rather than AWAY moves. This ability has dramatically improved my relationships. I have even noticed that different emotions present in unique ways and occur in different parts of my body. This helps me navigate painful emotions more quickly and effectively when they arise.

Learning to resist the struggle to ignore, solve or avoid unpleasant sensations and instead observe our emotions with curiosity is a skill most of us need to practise. But if we can learn to do it, it saves so much time and energy that can be better used for God's glory and our good!

Are you willing to have another go at tolerating a painful feeling? Think of another situation that will arouse a different negative emotion.

To begin with, you might only be able to tolerate a difficult emotion for a few seconds. Gradually build up your tolerance. If tolerating emotional pain is initially too hard, start with physical sensations like hunger or physical pain and build up to emotions.

Life felt so much easier when I discovered that each emotional ouch is very brief. It's a bit like having a filling at the dentist: nobody likes the pain, but knowing it'll soon pass allows you to wait it out without struggling. When you feel a strong emotion, simply stop and wait for a few minutes. Most emotions, if watched, will quickly lessen, allowing you to get on with doing what's important. However, expect comebacks: emotions return in waves, though always with a rise, a peak and a fall.

Here is a personalised script written by a friend. It might be useful to create your own as it combines a number of the techniques we've explored.

- Notice and name: *I'm noticing a feeling of anxiety. It's horrid, but I can allow this feeling—I don't have to struggle or get rid of it. It's not dangerous. It'll soon pass.*
- Observe the detail: *I can watch this, make room for it, and see what it does and where it is in my body. This is just*

a feeling. I am not my emotions—I am the observer. It's high in my chest. It's rhythmic and pounding. It feels like I can't swallow or breathe. It comes in waves. I can watch the rise and fall of each emotional wave.

- Come to your senses: *I can hear a car and see some dust. Right now, what's important is cooking supper for my son.*
- Expect comebacks: *I feel the emotion returning. That's okay—it's what emotions do. I'll watch it again.*

As you keep practising, you'll spot the feelings that you find hardest. Knowing this helps. Take courage and confide in someone else which feelings are tricky for you and which situations are likely to trigger painful feelings; it will probably help them to talk honestly with you. It changed everything the first time I told my husband that going to a party would be a massive struggle because of the jealousy I would feel!

Trusting Jesus

I pointed out earlier that even a gun to our head can't stop our emotions. It's no wonder then that when someone says things like, "Don't worry", "Don't be afraid", "Cheer up", it doesn't seem to help!

Yet Jesus gave emotional commands.

Do not worry. (Matthew 6:25)

Take heart. (John 16:33)

Don't be afraid. (John 6:20)

There are emotional commands elsewhere in Scripture too. We are told to...

- rejoice and give thanks in all circumstances (1 Thessalonians 5:16-18).
- think on what is good, honest and true (Philippians 4:8).
- weep with those who weep (Romans 12:15).
- grieve over sin (Matthew 5:4).

How can this work when we have so little control over what we feel and think?

Consider this.

A friend of mine was shoved aside by an obnoxious lady in a shop doorway. My friend was understandably furious. She thought, "I am always treated badly. Other people are so rude."

Then the shop assistant explained that the frantic customer had received a call to say her son had been badly injured. Instantly my friend's feelings changed from anger to compassion. The truth instantly changed how she felt.

The truth changes how we feel. Emotional commands are not pointless if the commanding person changes the truth about your situation—if he or she can change your mind or meet your need.

Jesus said:

> *I have told you these things, so that in me you may have peace. In this world you will have trouble. But take heart! I have overcome the world. (John 16:33)*

Jesus has changed things for us. Thankfully, in him we can think right, feel right and do right!

Pause for a Look in God's Mirror

Prayerfully read Ezekiel 36:25-27.

We often hurt when the worthless idols we have chosen let us down. Any object or activity that takes God's place is an idol. Good things become idols when they delight and excite us more than God. Bad things become idols when they soothe and consume us more than God.

Whether they seem like good or bad things in themselves, all idols will drive you MAD!

Consider: what are yours?

Idols are like the broken cisterns of Jeremiah 2:13. Instead of living water, we're trying to quench our thirst with moist mud. No wonder our MAD behaviours leave us parched and dehydrated.

But remember the man who said this to a thirsty woman:

> *Jesus answered, "Everyone who drinks this water will be thirsty again, but whoever drinks the water I give them will never thirst." (John 4:13-14)*

Ask the Spirit to soften your heart so that you experience God as more worthy and more satisfying than all of your idols. Then, right emotions will flow more often. Ask him for the courage to be more like Jesus in your emotional responses.

Song to sing: *Grace Awaiting Me* by EMU Music. But change the line "Grace is greater than our *failings*" to "Grace is greater than our *feelings*".

CHAPTER 8

THOUGHT SABOTEURS

I was walking with my daughter when I saw my husband. I ran to catch up with him. Between giggles, my daughter said, "That's not Dad! You should have gone to Specsavers!"

I believed what I saw, but outdated glasses fed me lies. My faulty lenses almost made me hug a stranger!

My mind is also a lens. Our mind is our control centre—the source of our beliefs and thoughts. It's the lens through which I make sense of God, myself and the world. Unfortunately, our belief lenses are often false or faulty. We acquire beliefs quickly, often early in life, and apply them rigidly. We find it hard to update them, and they rarely leave us completely.

Every situation I come across. Every person I meet. Every thought, feeling or idea. They're all viewed through my belief lenses. As a result, my beliefs can take control over what I do.

- If I believe people can't be trusted, I won't join a house group or be honest.

- If I believe I am doomed to fail, I won't try anything or use my gifts.
- If I believe I'm a victim, I'll be suspicious and won't notice kindness.
- If I believe I'm the clever one, I'll look down on others and refuse help.

I am the product of what I think. Yikes!

Jesus the Optician

Before you met Jesus, you were unable to see the truth of the gospel because you were blinded—you couldn't see the truth about what was right in front of you (2 Corinthians 4:4; Ephesians 4:18; Romans 1:21). You lived in darkness. But here is what happens when God breaks into an unbelieving heart:

> *For God, who said, "Let light shine out of darkness," made his light shine in our hearts to give us the light of the knowledge of God's glory displayed in the face of Christ.*
>
> *(2 Corinthians 4:6)*

As part of our spiritual birth, we receive new lenses and can finally see what is there. We can see the truth of God's word and accept what it says about Jesus. As believers, we can truthfully say, "I've seen the light"! The light of Jesus changes our minds about everything. Now we are able to see God, ourselves and the world rightly.

The problem is that even as Christians, we still get tempted to put on the old faulty glasses and navigate the world using our old beliefs. When we suffer, we're especially prone to reverting back to the lenses we acquired as children. Satan's desire is for you to forget that you have new vision!

This is why Paul says in Romans 12:2 that we are not to conform to the pattern of this world but to be transformed by the renewing of our minds. Renewed minds use God's word to see the world, themselves and others. Renewed minds recognise that the lenses acquired in childhood, through past experience or via the opinions of this world are inaccurate.

But this doesn't happen immediately. We have to learn to think like Jesus.

A Right Mind

I have been freshly impacted by the story of the demon-possessed man in Mark 5. Living alone among graves, he was tortured and helpless. All he could do was cry out and cut himself with stones.

Then along came Jesus.

When the people from the surrounding area heard that Jesus had freed the man, they couldn't resist a look:

> *When they came to Jesus, they saw the man who had been possessed by the legion of demons, sitting there, dressed and in his right mind; and they were afraid.*
>
> *(Mark 5:15)*

Among that crowd, I imagine a hopeless mother who had given up on her boy, hearing the gossip that said he was restored. I imagine her abandoning the meal she'd been cooking, leaving the pots bubbling, to sprint for the hills. Surely it couldn't be true. Surely her hopeless, helpless, tortured son was out of his mind, unreachable. I imagine her puffing up the hill and catching a first glimpse of her renewed boy—calm, dressed and smiling. What joy she would have felt to see this new creation! Her son, in his right mind, thirsty for the new life ahead.

Take a moment to feel my description of someone who has been gifted a right mind. That's what Jesus wants for you!

A right mind enables you to believe truth, whatever things look or feel like. A right mind produces right feelings, right actions and a right life.

Is your mind resisting this idea? Perhaps you are saying, "She doesn't know how I think. She doesn't know what I've been through. She doesn't know how negative I am. She doesn't know how broken I am."

If your mind is doing that, let God speak to your heart with Paul's words:

> *But we have the mind of Christ. (1 Corinthians 2:16)*

If you are a follower of Jesus, you *have* the mind of Christ. You have the right lenses at your disposal!

Setting Your Mind

So how do we learn to think like Jesus? How do we get a Christlike mind? Colossians 3:1-2 gives us our instructions:

> *Since, then, you have been raised with Christ, set your hearts on things above, where Christ is, seated at the right hand of God. Set your minds on things above, not on earthly things.*

Or here's Romans 8:5:

> *Those who live according to the flesh have their minds set on what the flesh desires; but those who live in accordance with the Spirit have their minds set on what the Spirit desires.*

The first thing we need to think about is where we are setting our minds.

Right now, my mind is set on a spring break in Marrakech. I read endlessly about the place and seek out people who've been. I'm obsessed with the idea of going. As a result, I'm excited. My thoughts frequently drift to the imagined colour and sunshine.

When my husband had the audacity to ask, "What about Spain?" I was not impressed.

We change our minds by setting our minds on things above. We need to be obsessed with the right things—to intentionally fill our minds with the glorious gospel of grace, not just once but every day. We need to know God's word better than we know the quotes from our favourite film or novel! Then, in every situation, our natural disposition will be to think like Christ; and our right thoughts, beliefs and desires will be revealed in our camera behaviour.

- If I feel guilty, I'll know I'm forgiven, so I won't blame or descend in shame.
- If someone criticises me, I'll know I'm justified by Christ, so I won't be defensive.
- If I'm offered a promotion, I'll have nothing to prove, so I'll consider it wisely.

- If I'm worried about my health, I'll know that God has numbered my days, and feel peace.

If we believe right, we'll think right, and we'll respond right. If we think like Jesus, we'll respond like Jesus.

The City of My Soul

I love John Bunyan's idea, in his allegorical novel *The Holy War,* about the city of Mansoul. He tells us that Eye Gate and Ear Gate are the easiest places for enemy saboteurs to enter the city. It's another way of understanding what it means to set your mind on something. Do you realise that the things you allow into your mind through your eyes and ears can have a huge power to influence you—for good or bad?

Here's a demonstration... I know what you'll be thinking in two seconds!

Mary had a little...?

If you were educated in the English-speaking world, I bet "lamb" popped into your head?

I set you up! I made you think about a lamb. It wasn't your choice.

Most of us don't know when we first learned that nursery rhyme. Our minds have hoovered it up and stored it, along with a huge amount of other content that later pops up as uninvited thoughts or pictures and grabs our attention when we least expect it.

This doesn't matter when it's a nursery rhyme about a lamb, but what about other examples? If we watch films with violence and sexually immoral content, our mouths will speak it, and our behaviour will reflect it. If we listen to gossip and consume endless social-media content, our minds will become conformed to it.

This is why Philippians 4:8 urges us...

> *Finally, brothers and sisters, whatever is true, whatever is noble, whatever is right, whatever is pure, whatever is lovely, whatever is admirable—if anything is excellent or praiseworthy—think about such things.*

We can't delete what's already stored in our minds, although in a minute I'll show you how to manage it. However, it's a good idea to stop and consider what we are letting in to the city of our minds in the first place.

We can't control everything that we see and hear. But we can choose to let in more of what's good and less of what's bad. We can set our minds on what is above, inviting the Holy Spirit to show us what right beliefs and right actions are.

How to Treat Your Thoughts

Without my permission, delivery men bang on my front door to throw in a parcel. It frightens the life out of me. Often thoughts arrive like that, don't they? They're unexpected, and sometimes they hurt and frighten us.

Even if we set our minds on Christ, we still can't control everything that comes into our head, so what on earth can we do when an unwanted thought intrudes on us?

I can't stop a delivery man catching me unawares. However, I don't need to offer him a drink. I don't invite him in. I don't cook an extravagant meal and enjoy his company.

While we can't stop an unwanted thought jumping into our minds when we least expect it, we can choose what we *do* with those thoughts.

Often, our problem is that we actually like our sinful thoughts, so we entertain them, playing host to them. We replay, go over, embellish or get consumed by a thought chain. Being entangled in a thorny thought bush can feel energising or exciting! It might give me a reason not to do something I don't want to do or justify an action I know to be wrong. At other times, going over and over a train of thoughts might soothe me when I'm anxious or prevent difficult feelings. For example, ruminating about what might go wrong distracts me from the fear I feel and may protect me from disappointment if things indeed don't work out.

Imagine that the thought "I really don't like that woman" pops into your head. How might you entertain that thought? How might you enjoy its company, pulling out the stops to give it a good time? Maybe like this: "I don't like her. I don't like the way she prays. I think she's shallow. Her clothes are expensive. I think she's a bit of a flirt. She reminds me of that other woman I don't like. I can't help it. I'm sure others don't like her either. I'll ask a few friends what they think..."

What about the thought "I am going to lose my job"? You might go over all the reasons why you fall short at work. You might replay all of your past mistakes. Or you might come up with the many reasons why you shouldn't be made redundant, or the reasons why other people should lose their jobs first.

At best, these mind activities are time-wasting and will wind us into an anxious or angry frenzy. At worst, they'll lead us into sinful words and actions.

Instead of entertaining our unhelpful thoughts and getting entangled, we need to take them captive!

> *We demolish arguments and every pretension that sets itself up against the knowledge of God, and we take captive every thought to make it obedient to Christ.*
>
> *(2 Corinthians 10:5)*

Some Christians feel frightened by the darkness of their thinking and get entangled with thoughts like, "What sort of person has thoughts like that? What if others knew? I am disgusting, unforgivable." They forget that we're all messy inside, and they feel embarrassed or ashamed about their dark, sinful or negative thoughts. Alternatively, they strive to suppress these thoughts. They believe that this is what Paul means by "take captive every thought".

But denying and suppressing unwanted thoughts is exhausting and distracting, and leads to dishonesty and defeat—which is the opposite of what Paul wants for the believers he is writing to. He wants us to live with the freedom a right mind offers.

Paul's imagery is of a military operation. Each enemy soldier needs to be spotted and taken captive in order to stop them from sabotaging us. And what are these enemy soldiers? Paul is talking about anything that is "against the knowledge of God". It goes back to having a right mind and knowing what God wants. Taking every thought captive means seeing it for what it truly is, in the light of the gospel.

Patrolling the Battlefield

Let's try some different ways to disentangle from our unhelpful, distracting or sinful thoughts so they don't cause us to stumble. At first these ideas might seem silly, but persevere—these tools will loosen the power of your thoughts and stop them controlling your actions.

First, try this simple exercise: wave your hands in the air while saying in your mind, "I can't lift my hands." Realise that you can control your actions regardless of what you're thinking. You can't control your thoughts, but you can defy them.

1. NOTICE, NAME, REFOCUS

The first step to managing a thought or belief is simply to notice and name it:

- I am noticing I am having a thought that she doesn't like me.
- I am noticing a distracting thought about what I need to do this evening.
- I am noticing the belief that I am stupid and will always fail.

Then, refocus using your senses. What can I hear right now? What and who is it important for me to focus on? Move towards that.

2. WRITE OUT YOUR THOUGHTS

Writing out thoughts is useful when you're getting the

hang of noticing and naming. Seeing your thoughts on paper diminishes their power and helps you spot your most frequent unhelpful thoughts. I have a list of mine on the wall of my office! When I notice one pop into my head, I simply nod at the list and get on with my work. It sounds bizarre, but it saves so much struggle, time and energy.

3. INTERVIEW YOUR THOUGHTS

When you've noticed a thought, ask it my favourite questions:

- If I believe this thought as the absolute truth, what will I do? Will that be a TOWARDS or AWAY move?
- Is this thought useful or helpful to me in this moment?
- When was the first time I had this thought? Is this an "old glasses" story?

I have written those questions on post-it notes in my car, kitchen and office!

4. CONFESS YOUR THOUGHTS

If you have a recurring sinful thought chain, you can confess it and ask for the Spirit's help to change your mind. Speaking to a trustworthy friend or sensible church leader about what's going on within your inner life is another way of noticing and naming. Naming thoughts, writing them out, speaking them to others or confessing them to the Lord demolishes their power to control your actions.

5. GIVE YOUR MIND A ROLE

Your mind is not separate from you, but it can still be helpful to think of it as being like a distinct part of you that you can notice. By practising your STOMPs and coming to your senses, have you noticed what your mind is like? Do you have a chatterbox mind—one that is always commenting on what's happening? Or is your mind like an interfering parent, always giving advice? Perhaps it's a bully, always pointing out your faults, or a pessimistic radio, forever shouting warnings.

Most people find it helpful to respond to their mind's role by saying something like "Thanks mind, I already know my faults," or "Thank you, Doom Radio, for trying to help."

6. NOTICE AND NAME YOUR MIND ACTIVITIES

What activities does your mind always come back to? Perhaps it's some of these:

- *Worrying:* dwelling on things that frighten you or cause you concern.
- *Ruminating:* going over and over something that is historical or out of your control.
- *Problem-solving:* thinking of all the ways you might be able to solve an unsolvable problem.
- *Catastrophising:* imagining the worst possible scenario.
- *Judging:* dwelling on the faults of others and how they are less good than you.
- *Resenting:* dwelling on how you've been wronged, treated unfairly or victimised.
- *Selfing:* being self-focused; dwelling on all that's wrong or right with you.
- *Regretting:* dwelling on past experiences.
- *Futuring:* thinking about all that may or may not happen in the future.

When you catch yourself getting entangled in one or more of these mind activities, simply name the mind activity by saying, "Here I am worrying." Then use your senses to reconnect with the outside world, asking yourself, "What and who is important right now?"

Try this for extra practice. Intentionally bring to mind a concern, something you're worrying about or dwelling on. Go over and over it on purpose. Then stop. Name it: "Here I am worrying." Come to your senses and do what's important.

Now do the same with a difficult situation from the past. Practising intentionally helps you notice more quickly when you get entangled in real time.

7. NAME YOUR STORIES

Often painful situations hang about in our minds, making us vulnerable to bitterness, rage or resentment. Our minds get drawn back to them again and again. We can waste hours going over the same material when we could be looking up and out.

Here is a helpful technique for these consuming mind themes. Get a piece of paper and brainstorm all the thoughts, images and memories associated with the painful situation. Write them all down, in any order.

Then fold the paper in two so that it's like a book. Imagine that the situation is a novel—give it a dramatic title like "The Appalling Neighbour" or "I'll Never Get Better". Write this title on the cover of your book.

Each day, allow yourself ten minutes once or twice a day to carefully read aloud what you've written. Notice the feelings and tolerate them, as described in the last chapter.

Then put it away in your bag or pocket. For the rest of the day, when this situation pops into your mind, simply say, "Thank you, mind, I know the Appalling Neighbour story." Come to your senses and get on.

Other stories are linked to our old belief glasses. For me, it's the "Rejection" story, when I get left out or feel ignored. Then there's the "Terrible Mum" story, when I feel I've failed as a parent. My husband has the "I Have Nothing to Say" and the "Everything Will Go Wrong" stories.

What are your favourite mind stories? You might not recognise them yet, but as you get used to noticing your thoughts, you'll start to spot certain themes. Notice these stories as they pop up and name them: "Here's the Rejection story again."

The Mind of Christ

As we consume more and more of God's truth, we will start to see situations and challenges from God's point of view. Our old lenses look in and down. But wearing God's glasses, we will see the needs and interests of others, making us more like Jesus.

Ask Jesus to be your vision so that everything but him will count for nothing. Then you'll believe what he believes, care where he cares, hurt where he hurts and do what he wants done. Then you'll have the mind of Christ.

With the mind of Jesus and the Spirit's empowering, we can buy beef even when our thoughts shout "Lamb!"

Pause for a Look in God's Mirror

Prayerfully read John 4:47-50.

Imagine that distressed father, begging Jesus for the life of his son. When Jesus spoke, the man took him at his word. No questions, no doubts. Imagine the difference that made. Imagine that same father rushing home to his son, knowing he was alive.

You can't take God at his word unless you know what he says. So...

Write out three things God says in the Bible about himself, you and others. Then ask yourself, "What would change if I really believed these truth statements and lived accordingly?"

- How would your prayer life change?
- How would the way you relate to others change?
- What would you do more of or stop doing?

Ask the Spirit to reveal the faulty beliefs you hold and the thought themes you entertain that dishonour God or lead to sinful and unhelpful patterns of behaviour.

Are you willing to truthfully pray these lines from the hymn by Kate Barclay Wilkinson?

May the mind of Christ, my Saviour,
Live in me from day to day,
By his love and power controlling
All I do and say.

Song to sing: *Be Thou My Vision*

CHAPTER 9

RACING WITH OTHERS

As a child my favourite film was *The Wizard of Oz*. If you can, take a peek at "We're Off to See the Wizard" on YouTube and share my joy!

Arm in arm, four needy people skip along the yellow brick road. The tin man is emotionally numb, the lion has an anxiety disorder and the scarecrow is not very bright. As a homeless orphan, Dorothy has attachment problems and struggles to trust within close relationships.

Despite their brokenness, when trials come, they encourage each other to hope in someone who is sufficiently powerful to heal their wounds and solve their problems. Their hope enables them to courageously persevere.

Unfortunately, the wizard of Oz does not prove to be trustworthy... But our God is! In every other respect, this is a great picture of what we should be like as Christian siblings.

Being God's People

If asked what a church is, most non-believers would say it's a religious building. This is not what the Bible means by church. The word "church" is a translation of the Greek word *ekklesia*, which essentially means "called-out ones". Church is not a building but a group of believers who have been called out of the rat race into a radically different, alternative way of life. United around Jesus. No favourites. No outsiders. No scapegoats.

Scripture describes the church as a body. What a great picture! We all have one for reference.

> *But God has put the body together, giving greater honour to the parts that lacked it, so that there should be no division in the body, but that its parts should have equal concern for each other. If one part suffers, every part suffers with it; if one part is honoured, every part rejoices with it. Now you are the body of Christ, and each one of you is a part of it. (1 Corinthians 12:24-27)*

Local churches are supposed to function like a body—which means working together and caring for each other. I sometimes work with people who have severe movement disorders. Their limbs refuse to work in conjunction with the rest of the body, and sadly, even the simplest task becomes impossible. Likewise, in the church, every member matters. If we don't work together, the entire body is negatively affected. But when we worship God and serve each other—loving together, rejoicing together and suffering together—it's beautiful!

The church is also compared to a family. We are brothers and sisters in Christ, children of God, the family of believers, God's household.

When I think of my body, I'm reminded of its flaws, and

when many of us picture a family, we think of hurt and dysfunction. Bodies and families are tarnished by the Fall—yet the design idea is obvious. Church is not a shop we visit when there's a special offer. Church is not a football match where a few play while the rest watch and criticise. Church is not a concert where we get entertained or made to feel good. Church is not a vending machine where we choose what we'd like and go on our way. Church is a body. Church is a family. We are supposed to help each other run the race.

The Beauty and the Beast

Scripture also tells us that the church is the bride of Christ (Ephesians 5:25-27; Revelation 21:2). He gave himself up to turn us into a beautiful bride! So our local church should be the place where we don't pretend. The place where we are honest about our failings and feelings. The place where forgiveness is a given.

If you're part of a biblical church, you'll have experienced what I call glimmer moments. Moments, however fleeting, when you've felt and loved what God intended for his body.

I feel it when my friend Mitzi and I chat over a latte about how God is changing us. It's when my friend Jo and I confess our mutual struggles and encourage each other to carry on. It's when my friend Marc and I weep and make up after a silly misunderstanding. It's when my church family sing of the grace of God and plead together for a hurting sibling. It's when I look around and see people of different cultures, ages and backgrounds chatting like the closest of friends.

Despite the equality and inclusion policies, and despite the "be kind" slogans and the heart-warming posts on Facebook, I don't find genuine love, inclusion, equality and forgiveness anywhere but in my local church!

Allow yourself a moment of grateful reflection. Do you know what a gift your church family is? Bring to mind as many church glimmer moments as you can. Write down all the times you've enjoyed running the race with others. The moments of true fellowship, emotional honesty, forgiveness and inclusion. Enhance them in your mind; feel them in your body. Thank God for each one as you remember.

But I know that for some readers, church hasn't been what God intended. Perhaps you've suffered great hurt within the body of believers. Perhaps you've been treated unfairly; you've felt betrayed when people have left the church suddenly without comment; you've been discouraged when the work is hard but some are doing nothing. Let's be honest: we all have moments that make us want to throw in the towel! It's so sad when rat-race behaviour plays out in the church.

However, when I take an honest look into my heart, I realise that I too have let people down. I've said hurtful and rude things. I've been the lazy one at church. I'm part of the problem!

Why on earth is my church so flawed? Why is this bride sometimes so ugly? The short answer is that it's full of people like me, with terrible thoughts, fallen feelings and dodgy desires. Yet this is God's plan: he puts us messy humans together, gifts us his Spirit and urges us to help each other become beautiful.

Let us hold unswervingly to the hope we profess, for he who promised is faithful. And let us consider how we may spur one another on towards love and good deeds, not giving up meeting together, as some are in the habit of doing, but encouraging one another—and all the more as you see the Day approaching. (Hebrews 10:23-25)

In this chapter we are going to consider how we may spur one another on towards love and good deeds, encouraging each other to hold unswervingly to the hope we profess.

Who You Are

For years, I wanted to be a wise, quietly spoken woman, gifted at craft and baking cakes. If you knew me, you'd find that hilarious. But I studied women like that, hoping that one day I'd be like them.

Now I realise that this is not what God wants. The metaphor of the body tells us that every part is different and every part is valued. The Spirit doesn't eradicate your personality and make you into another church member you admire. The church has one of those already. God makes us into the best version of ourselves—a perfect fit for the places and people he's designed us for.

We are designed to image *him*, not someone else. Anything less will diminish you and leave the church with a missing piece.

There's room for all of us in the church. But we'll do a better job of spurring one another on if we are aware of each other's gifts and weaknesses, and if we are able to have honest conversations about what we need from others in order to thrive.

The truth about me is that I'm passionate about Jesus and I love to speak out, often saying too much. I have big ideas and a big mouth. I find it easy to be bold, but often that makes me rush in and be rude and insensitive. I make big claims but then crumble in a heap of despair when I get it wrong.

My husband is reflective. He thinks it all through before he says or does anything. But sometimes he ponders too much, and that merges into avoidance. He puts off big conversations and often says too little, allowing people off the hook when they need to be challenged.

Consider who you are. What are your gifts, and what are your besetting weaknesses? What are your strengths, and how could you use them to help others? What thoughts, feelings and desires get in the way of you doing that? What struggles or vulnerabilities do you need others to know about in order for them to help you live for Jesus?

At the end of this chapter, you will find a tool called the four-part lens, which will help you take stock of some of these things and move forward. But first, here are four ways in which we can help each other to run the race—along with some thoughts on why they may be difficult and how we can get better at them.

Courageous Conversations

The Scriptures tell us to stir up one another to love and good works (Hebrews 10:24); to confess our faults to one another (James 5:16); to speak the truth in love (Ephesians 4:15, 25); and to admonish one another

(Romans 15:14; Colossians 3:16). If you're naturally inclined to please people and avoid conflict, you'll find all of this hard! We need courage.

As Christian siblings, our key responsibility is to help each other become more like Jesus. Biblical love isn't a fake smile and a peck on the cheek. It isn't complaining about someone behind their back or in your mind. It's telling them the truth in love so they can change, and having the courage to accept the same back.

Biblical love calls us to be emotionally honest about ourselves and to have courageous conversations with others. This might trigger negative feelings like anxiety or self-doubt. But we are called to do what's right despite our bad feelings.

What thoughts, feelings and desires make you avoid courageous conversations?

Giving Attention

Wherever we go, there are two heart postures to choose from. I can say, "Here I am", expecting people to notice and meet my needs. With this attitude, I'll be disappointed if I'm not the centre of attention, or if I'm not made to feel worthy or important. Alternatively, I can say, "There you are". I can seek someone to love rather than seeking people to love me. This is God's heart.

We are told to have the same mindset as Christ Jesus in our relationships (Philippians 2:5). Jesus had every right to announce, "Here I am", because he is God! He is the Creator—the way, the truth and the life. He is the beginning and the end. He is the one and only perfect person. And yet Jesus chose to be made nothing for the sake of others.

What thoughts, feelings and desires turn you into a "Here I am" person, focusing on your own needs instead of others? Where do you long to have the mind of Christ?

Being a Comforter

I have a friend whose daughter died in terrible circumstances. She told me that people would sometimes cross the street to avoid having to talk about her grief. I've heard similar stories countless times. When someone is in distress, it's natural to feel helpless. But if we're not careful, our helplessness will make us say invalidating platitudes or run away to escape our own discomfort.

Here are some things we might do to escape our bad feelings. Do you recognise any?

- Lying. "It'll be fine. These things always come right."
- Offering simplistic solutions without listening.
- Trying to empathise dishonestly. "I know exactly how you feel" (when you don't).
- Being overly positive. "Don't forget all the positive times. Look on the bright side."
- Giving the impression that emotions are abnormal. "Calm down. Don't upset yourself."
- Avoiding or ignoring the person.

Whatever the reasons for the person's distress, our starting point needs to be humble compassion as an equally messed-up person. If this person's real problem is sin or a negative pattern of behaviour, there might be a later time when a courageous conversation is needed—but whatever the problem is, we'll get the best response if we first listen and comfort.

Here are five easy steps for being a godly comforter.

1. *Notice your own heart.* "I am feeling anxious and helpless." Or, "I have an urge to tell them what to do or blame them for their stupidity."
2. *Listen, and label* the feeling they're expressing, even if it's not what you'd feel or you don't understand their response. "It sounds like you feel angry and frustrated."
3. *Validate their emotional pain,* even if you don't agree with their conclusions or response. Emotional pain is part of being human, and it hurts! It shows that we care about something. Help them work out what their pain shows they care about. "You are anxious about this because you want to honour God." "You dread an empty nest because you are a good mum."
4. *Seek the truth.* What lies are easy for the person to believe in this situation? Perhaps it's "No one likes me," "This church is lucky to have me," or "I have nothing to offer." To help the person spot the unhelpful lies, it can help to write out their thoughts as they disclose them. Seeing them on paper adds clarity and diminishes their power to overwhelm. Together, take a compassionate look at the thoughts and feelings that underlie the hurt. Ask the Spirit to renew your minds and show you the truth about the situation.
5. *Move TOWARDS.* What could you both do in this situation to move towards God's values despite the painful feelings?

Being Hard to Offend

When you feel upset in response to another person, take the time to notice and name it within your mind before you respond. Allow the feeling to be there. Remember that most emotions are fleeting.

Often, you'll feel hurt because of your history, your faulty beliefs and your emotional landmines. Just because you feel offended, it doesn't mean the person wanted to give offence. Feeling rejected isn't the same as being rejected. Often, it's best to go away and reflect in prayer or chat to a friend or church leader before you accuse. If, after careful reflection, you think the other person is in the wrong, you can then take courage and speak gently to them.

When someone has sinned against you, it is wise to approach them using "I feel" language. For example, if my husband is irritable with me, he is more likely to apologise if I say, "I felt hurt by the way you spoke to me," than if I say, "You're always so irritable." It's better to say, "I felt left out today," than it is to say, "You always ignore me."

If someone responds disproportionately or in a way that is childish or unexpected, you've probably unknowingly triggered one of their old stories. Try not to take it personally.

Racing Together

So much recent research has proved that we are not designed to be alone. Social isolation makes people physically and mentally ill, reduces quality of life and even causes premature death.

The local church has been ordained by God so that nobody has to race alone. We each have an inner mess; too often, our strengths clash, and our needs stay hidden and therefore unmet. But we can wrap ourselves up in Jesus and be empowered by his Spirit!

Let's commit to proving Jesus' worth by relating to each other in an emotionally honest way. Then, our churches will show the radically different alternative culture that God intended—and people outside of the church will be bursting through our doors to escape the rat race.

Bringing It All Together: The Four-Part Lens

I'd like to introduce to you a tool called a four-part lens. I'll show you how to use it in three different ways. Like a camera lens, it gives me a more objective perspective on my own behaviour. It helps me to know what change to pray for and to stay in step with the Spirit.

Start by grabbing a large piece of paper. Divide it into four quadrants and label them like this:

AWAY MOVES	TOWARDS MOVES
SABOTEURS	VALUES

The bottom half of the box is what's happening inside you. Nobody can see it! Meanwhile, the top half of the box shows what can be seen on a camera—the actions and words that flow out of our hidden inner world. Remember, our camera behaviour is always driven and underpinned by our unseen inner life.

The bottom left is never pretty, but as Christians, we don't have to descend into a cycle of shame and defeat at the sight of this inner mess. Can you view the left-hand side of your lens with the Father's compassion? It hurts to be a fallen human. But we are being made new.

Here are three ways to use your four-part lens.

1. TO UNDERSTAND MY BEHAVIOUR

Start by using the tool to examine how you show up at church.

1. What values do you want to show at church? Fill in the Values quadrant.
2. On a camera, what would you be seen doing or saying if you're showing these values? Fill in the TOWARDS Moves box.
3. What thoughts, feelings and desires might show up to sabotage you? Fill in the Saboteurs section.
4. What would you be seen doing or saying under the influence of these saboteurs? Fill in the AWAY Moves quadrant.

Look at my example on the following page to help you.

Have a look at your lens. What do you notice? Does anything surprise or interest you?

Do you notice how the bottom two quadrants are connected? We hurt where we care. For example, fearing rejection might show that I value courage.

As you look at your clarifying lens, pray for the Spirit's continued help to disentangle and do what's right. Check back in chapters 7 and 8 to remember how to disentangle from those sneaky saboteurs.

AWAY MOVES	TOWARDS MOVES
Rushing away after church. Ignoring the less popular people. Pretending I'm fine when I'm not.	Inviting people to my house. Sitting with the less popular people. Telling someone how I really feel.
SABOTEURS	**VALUES**
Thoughts: I don't know how to do this. Feelings: Anxiety, fear of rejection. Desires: To show off.	Hospitality Acceptance Courage

2. TO REFLECT ON AN AWAY MOVE

Now we're going to use this tool to examine an AWAY move, again within the context of church. Take another piece of paper and divide it into the same four quadrants.

This time, start in the AWAY Moves quadrant. Write here something you have said or done that is inconsistent with your grace-race code of conduct.

My example is this: being rude at a church meeting. My camera behaviour was a big sigh, folded arms and an eye-roll in response to someone's comment.

Now complete the Saboteurs box. What thoughts, feelings and desires underpinned that response? Here are mine:

- Thoughts: It's not fair. I'm not being heard. What's the point? Nobody cares.
- Feelings: Frustration. Irritability. Shame.
- Desires: To walk out, give up.

Now move to the Values quadrant. What values would God like you to show in this context? For me, it's patience, self-control, kindness, acceptance.

Finally, what behaviours would overflow from these values? Write those in the final box. I would write, "Smiling, eye contact, praying for patience, open body language."

Using the tool like this improves our awareness. It helps us to notice and improve our gut responses. When we submit what we have noticed to the Spirit, it helps us become more like Jesus!

3. TO IMPROVE A RELATIONSHIP

Think of a relationship you'd like to improve or someone you find difficult.

1. Complete the Values box first. What values would God like you to show in this relationship?
2. Then the Saboteurs section. What thoughts, feelings or desires might show up to sabotage your good intentions?
3. Next, complete the AWAY Moves box. What behaviours might overflow from that inner content?
4. Finally, fill in some TOWARDS moves. What behaviours might overflow from God's values?

I use this tool so often that my husband has banned me from using paper scraps and serviettes to complete a four-part lens in public! You can use it to reflect on an AWAY move or to plan a TOWARDS move. You can use it as a couple, a family, a small group or a church. Use it to choose beautiful bride behaviour and identify ugly bride behaviours! You can even use it to understand someone else. When you see someone behave in a way you find confusing or hard, ask yourself what might be in their four-part lens—what difficult thoughts and feelings might underpin their response?

You can also use your lens to help yourself confess your faults to others. As we do, we'll gain an intimacy and compassion that comes from better understanding each other and seeing that, in the end, we're all much the same. Let's pray for the courage to be honest with each other as we link arms and run together to the grace-race finish line!

Pause for a Look in God's Mirror

Let's take a final pause.

Take notice of a few breaths. What thoughts and feelings are showing up as you ponder church life? Can you speak honestly with God about that?

Prayerfully consider the "one another" statements below. You could write them out. Ask yourself three questions for each one:

- What would be seen on a camera if I showed this value at church?
- How can I translate this into some small actions for this Sunday, this month, and this year?
- Am I willing to do that?

Love one another.
Live in harmony with one another.
Build up one another.
Accept one another.
Admonish one another.
Care for one another.
Bear one another's burdens.
Forgive one another.
Be patient with one another.
Be kind and compassionate to one another.
Teach one another.
Comfort one another.
Encourage one another.
Show hospitality to one another.
Pray for one another.
Confess your faults to one another.

Confess in prayer your church-related faults. Ask the Spirit to change your heart so you will be willing to change.

Song to sing: *We Declare* by EMU Music

THE HOME STRAIGHT

The marathon date is drawing close. Oscar Johnson has forgotten past injuries, and his confidence is growing with every training run. He's scoffing steak as if cows are going out of fashion, because protein is the fuel that energises and protects.

Now that Oscar is moving in the sweet spot, it feels natural to run. With his eye on the medal, he's paying careful attention to his remaining training weeks. I hope there won't be too many race saboteurs to distract him, but I know he'll make it. I'm looking forward to seeing his well-deserved medal. Then it'll all feel worth it.

As I write the final paragraphs of this book, I'd love to tell you that I've cracked it—that if you practise my STOMPs, you'll never again struggle with difficult thoughts about yourself and others or feel overwhelmed by big feelings. If only! Sadly, I've had a terrible weekend. Yesterday I entertained some horribly impatient and judgmental thoughts and said some unkind and hurtful things to my long-suffering husband. I got entangled yet again.

But the race is not over.

In Christ, you and I are the apple of God's eye. We have his acceptance. Jesus has taken your failure, guilt and shame and is praying for you. You have the Holy Spirit to energise and sustain you. You just have to consume the meaty protein of God's word, stay in the sweet spot... and fix your eyes on the finish line.

I am a regular visitor to Starbucks coffee shops. Usually an extra-hot latte tastes pretty good. However, there's a Starbucks where my latte tastes truly amazing—better than in any other place. There's nothing different about this shop—in fact, it's often busier and grubbier than my usual places. It's the shop's location that changes everything... It's at Gatwick Airport!

At the airport Starbucks, even when the coffee is badly made and the barista scowls at me, I always drink with a smile on my face and hope in my heart. Why? Because at the airport Starbucks, I know I'll soon be somewhere better by far!

When the road is bumpy and the saboteurs are tangling us up, let's remember our goal—the final destination that is better than our messy hearts can imagine.

One day, you'll be free of inner struggles. One day, you'll be restored to the person you were designed to be. One day, you'll see Jesus face to face and hear your Saviour say, "Well done, good and faithful servant". This is the hope that makes everything taste better.

Forgetting what is behind and straining towards what is ahead, I press on towards the goal to win the prize for which God has called me heavenwards in Christ Jesus.

(Philippians 3:13-14)

Thank you for journeying with me in this book. I hope that sharing my inner mess will enable you to share yours. I look forward to meeting you in glory, where we'll all be free of mess—and psychologists will be redundant.

Song to sing: *Yet Not I But Through Christ in Me* by CityAlight

A Daily Look in God's Mirror

Hopefully you've enjoyed your looks in the mirror at the end of each chapter! Here is a daily mirror page that you can use again and again.

Bring to mind a verse of the Bible to ponder as you start the day. Commit your day to the Lord and ask the Spirit to help you pay careful attention as you run the grace race for another day.

Complete a STOMP. (See pages 73-74.)

Think through your day, planning a couple of TOWARDS moves to complete. You could scribble out a four-part lens if you need to clarify something.

Sing aloud to a worship song.

Choose three Cs to include in your schedule today. (See pages 86-87.)

Finally, come to your senses.

> *This is the day the LORD has made;*
> *We will rejoice and be glad in it. (Psalm 118:24, NKJV)*

ACKNOWLEDGEMENTS

This book would not exist if it wasn't for my friend Andrew Bunt. It was he who read the first pages of my ramblings and introduced me to The Good Book Company. Thank you, Andrew, for being a consistent and supportive book buddy from proposal to completion. You will always be my most famous friend!

I am grateful to Lauren Densham and Seren Boyd, who have encouraged my writing hobby for nearly a decade. It was both of them who suggested I try my hand at Christian non-fiction. I'm glad I did.

Thank you to all of those within my church family at Storrington Chapel who have prayed about or shown an interest in this book. Special thanks to Gerald, Mitzi and Cheryl, who have been consistent encouragers on this project, and to Ali Lutte-Elliott, my favourite clinical psychologist. Thank you for rescuing me when I was overwhelmed with difficult thoughts and feelings while writing the difficult thoughts and feelings chapters.

Last but not least, a massive shout-out to Katy Morgan, who had a vision for this book before I did and has been a reliable, patient and kind friend to me throughout the writing process, as well as a brilliant editor.

BIBLICAL | RELEVANT | ACCESSIBLE

At The Good Book Company we are dedicated to helping Christians and local churches grow. We believe that God's growth process always starts with hearing clearly what he has said to us through his timeless and flawless word—the Bible.

Ever since we opened our doors in 1991, we have been striving to produce resources that are biblical, relevant, and accessible. By God's grace, we have grown to become an international publisher, encouraging ordinary Christians of every age and stage and every background and denomination to live for Christ day by day and equipping churches to grow in their knowledge of God, their love for one another, and the effectiveness of their outreach.

Call one of our friendly team for a discussion of your needs or visit one of our local websites for more information on the resources and services we provide.

Your friends at The Good Book Company

thegoodbook.com | thegoodbook.co.uk
thegoodbook.com.au | thegoodbook.co.nz